THE SCOTTISH MASON

AND

THE MASON WORD

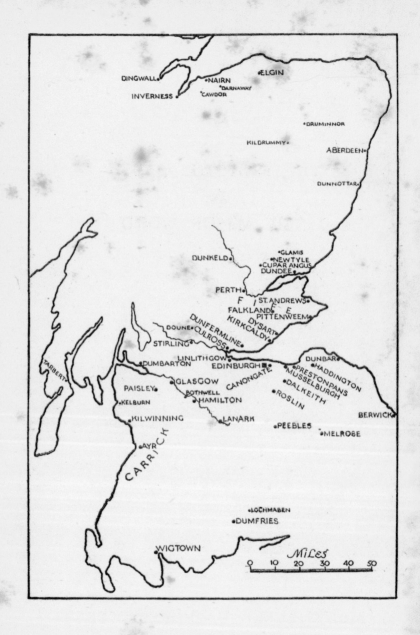

THE SCOTTISH MASON
AND
THE MASON WORD

BY

DOUGLAS KNOOP, M.A., Hon.A.R.I.B.A.

Professor of Economics in the University of Sheffield
P.M. Quatuor Coronati Lodge, No. 2076, London

AND

G. P. JONES, M.A., Litt.D.

Lecturer in Economic History in the University of Sheffield

MANCHESTER UNIVERSITY PRESS

1939

Published by the University of Manchester at
THE UNIVERSITY PRESS (H. M .McKechnie, M.A., Secretary)
8–10, Wright Street, Manchester, 15

PREFACE

OF the two studies printed in this book, the second, stimulated by the discovery of the *Graham MS.* at the end of 1936, was prepared first. The form which it finally took was determined by Douglas Knoop's appointment to give the Prestonian Lecture for 1938 on "The Mason Word." The Lecture is printed here unaltered, from the type of a pamphlet issued for private circulation in the spring of 1938. The other study, which is mainly concerned with the history of the Scottish building industry in the sixteenth and seventeenth centuries, incidentally attempts to explain why the Mason Word, as an operative institution, was found in Scotland and not in England, and what were the peculiar conditions which made its establishment and development in Scotland possible. This study of the Scottish Mason, begun as a short paper for communication to the Quatuor Coronati Lodge, has grown to such dimensions that only certain parts of it, somewhat rearranged in order, will ultimately appear in *A.Q.C.* under the title "Prolegomena to the Mason Word." The full paper, with its numerous notes and references, as printed here, provides not only a setting and a background for the study of the Mason Word, which is of special interest to Freemasons, but also a short history of the Scottish building industry, which we venture to hope may make a wider appeal.

We are greatly indebted to our colleague, Douglas Hamer, Lecturer in English Literature in the University, for valuable suggestions and helpful criticism, more especially in connection with the study of the MasonWord. We have also to thank our colleague, W. H. Wilcockson, Lecturer in Geology in the University, for advice on certain geological matters; the officials of the General Register House, and of the City Chamberlain's Department, Edinburgh, for their courtesy in facilitating our inspection of

v

certain manuscripts; Dr. J. Gilbart Smyly, Librarian of Trinity College, Dublin, for the information which he has kindly given us about two manuscripts in his keeping; Mr. A. L. Miller, for kindly supplying us with a copy of certain pages of the Mark Book of the Lodge of Aberdeen; Mr. David B. Morris, Town Clerk of Stirling, Professor W. R. Scott, Dr. W. Douglas Simpson and the Rev. Dr. J. H. Cockburn, for drawing our attention to certain sources of information, which we might otherwise have overlooked; our colleague, A. G. Pool, for reading the proofs; and Mr. H. M. McKechnie, Secretary of the Manchester University Press, for his advice and unfailing help.

D. K.
G. P. J.

The University,
Sheffield,
March, 1939.

CONTENTS

CONTENTS

LIST OF ABBREVIATED REFERENCES

A.Q.C.	.	*Ars Quatuor Coronatorum.*
Aberdeen	.	*Extracts from the Council Register of the Burgh of Aberdeen.*
Ayr	.	*Ayr Burgh Accounts, 1534–1624.*
Bain	.	E. Bain, *Merchant and Craft Guilds. A History of the Aberdeen Incorporated Trades.*
Cal. Doc. Scot.	.	*Calendar of Documents relating to Scotland.*
Cawdor	.	*The Book of the Thanes of Cawdor.*
Cruikshank	.	J. Cruikshank, *Sketch of the Incorporation of Masons.*
Cupar	.	*Rental Book of the Cistercian Abbey of Cupar-Angus.*
Edinburgh	.	*Extracts from the Records of the Burgh of Edinburgh.*
Exch. R.	.	*Exchequer Rolls of Scotland.*
Fleming	.	D. Hay Fleming, "The Accounts of Dr. Alexander Skene . . . relating to the extensive repairs of the College buildings . . . 1683–1690," *Proc. Soc. Antiq. Scot.,* 1919–20.
Glasgow	.	*Extracts from the Records of the Burgh of Glasgow.*
H. and W.	.	R. K. Hannay and G. P. H. Watson, *The Building of the Parliament House* (Extracted from the Thirteenth Volume of the Book of the Old Edinburgh Club, May 1924).
Henderson	.	J. M. Henderson, *Scottish Reckonings of Time, Money, Weights and Measures* (Historical Association of Scotland).
Inverness	.	*Records of Inverness.*
Lanark	.	*Extracts from the Records of the Burgh of Lanark.*
Laws	.	*Ancient Laws and Customs of the Burghs of Scotland, 1424–1707.*
Lyon	.	D. Murray Lyon, *History of the Lodge of Edinburgh (Mary's Chapel), No. 1.* (Tercentenary Edition.)
M.o.W A/cs.	.	Edinburgh Register House: Master of Works Accounts.
M. and R.	.	David Macgibbon and Thomas Ross, *The Castellated and Domestic Architecture of Scotland.*
Miller	.	A. L. Miller, *Notes on the Early History and Records of The Lodge, Aberdeen.*
Misc. Lat..	.	*Miscellanea Latomorum.*
Murray	.	Alfred A. A. Murray, "Freeman and Cowan, with special reference to the Records of Lodge Canongate Kilwinning," *A.Q.C.,* xxi.
Mylne	.	R. S. Mylne, *The Master Masons to the Crown of Scotland.*

LIST OF ABBREVIATED REFERENCES

O.E.D. .	.	*Oxford English Dictionary.*
Reg. P.C.	.	*Register of the Privy Council of Scotland.*
Stirling .	.	*Extracts from the Records of the Royal Burgh of Stirling, 1519–1666.*
Strathmore	.	*The Book of Record, a diary by Patrick, First Earl of Strathmore, and other documents relating to Glamis Castle, 1684–1689.*
Treas. A/cs.	.	*Accounts of the Lord High Treasurer of Scotland.*
Wallace-James .	.	R. E. Wallace-James, "The Minute Book of the Aitchison's Haven Lodge, 1598–1764," *A.Q.C.*, xxiv.

LOCATION OF DOCUMENTS QUOTED WITHOUT REFERENCES

Dunkeld Bridge Account, 1510–16. Mylne, 18–29.

Falkland Statutes, 1636. A. W. Laurie, *History of Freemasonry*, 1859, 445 *folg.*

Panmure House Building Contract, 1666. Mylne, 153–4.

Schaw Statutes, 1598 and 1599. Lyon, 9–14.

Tron Kirk (Edinburgh) Building Account, 1635–38. Edinburgh City Chamberlain's Department: bound volume of old accounts.

NOTE ON SCOTTISH MONEY

All figures relating to Scottish wage rates, contract prices and monetary penalties, quoted in this book, are in terms of pounds Scots, except where sterling is especially indicated.

The following table, based on Henderson, shows the number of pennies Scots equal to 1*d.* sterling at certain dates:

1390	.	.	.	2*d.*	1560	.	.	.	5*d.*
1451	.	.	.	2*d.*	1565	.	.	.	6*d.*
1456	.	.	.	3*d.*	1579	.	.	.	8*d.*
1467	.	.	.	3½*d.*	1597	.	.	.	10*d.*
1483	.	.	.	3½*d.*	1601–1700	.	.	.	12*d.*

THE SCOTTISH MASON

THE SCOTTISH MASON

THE day has not yet come when a comprehensive history of the Scottish mason can be written, and the early development of Scottish masonry, in consequence, must remain obscure and doubtful in many points. In this paper, therefore, we attempt only a preliminary survey on the basis of the evidence so far available and known to us, trusting that our study will help in clearing the ground. For reasons to be explained shortly, we are compelled to treat mainly of the sixteenth and seventeenth centuries. Those two centuries, however, constitute a period of great interest for masonic students, as it is possible to establish the existence in those times of certain features of Scottish operative masonry—such as the system of entered apprenticeship; the organisation which, for want of a better term, we call the "territorial lodge"; and the institution of the Mason Word—all of which appear to have exerted special influence on the subsequent development of speculative masonry.

We may begin, as is fitting, by acknowledging the labours of our predecessors—far fewer than we could have wished —in the field, and by indicating the sources at their disposal and ours. In the first place, there exist various histories of the older Scottish Lodges.[1] Secondly, there are three contributions of a more general character, dating from the late nineteenth century, by R. F. Gould,[2] by D. Macgibbon and T. Ross,[3] and by R. S Mylne.[4] The first is largely concerned with the histories of the older Scottish lodges; the second supplements a detailed architectural study with various particulars from building accounts and other documents; the third traces somewhat discursively, in a large

---

[1] E.g., Lyon, Miller and Wallace-James.
[2] *History of Freemasonry*, especially chapter viii, on Early British Freemasonry in Scotland.
[3] M. and R., especially the Appendix to vol. v.
[4] *The Master Masons to the Crown of Scotland.*

and sumptuous volume, the development of the administration of royal building operations in Scotland, a branch of administration with which several of the author's ancestors had a long and honourable connection. Thirdly, there are recent papers by Lionel Vibert [1] and J. A. Grantham; [2] the former is concerned to a considerable extent with English conditions, and the latter treats in the main of the origins of the Grand Lodge of Scotland.

Sources.—In comparison with England, the Northern Kingdom—more thinly populated, economically more backward, and with the central authority less developed and secure—is poor in records, and the number of records has also been reduced by shipwreck. [3] The *Exchequer Rolls of Scotland* and the *Accounts of the Lord High Treasurer of Scotland* are indeed voluminous; but the information to be gleaned from them, interesting so far as it goes, cannot compare, either in amount or importance, with that to be extracted from the long series of Exchequer Accounts in the Public Record Office in London. The Edinburgh Register House has a useful collection of accounts relating to Edinburgh Castle, Holyroodhouse, Linlithgow Palace and other royal buildings; [4] but these are of comparatively late date, from 1529 to 1679, and far less copious and instructive than the records available for the study of building history in England and Wales. Similarly, the *Register of the Privy Council of Scotland* [5] and the *Calendar of Documents relating to Scotland* are less informative than the comparable English rolls and state papers.

Monastic, ecclesiastical and collegiate records are

---

[1] "The Early Freemasonry of England and Scotland", *A.Q.C.*, xliii (1930).

[2] "Early Freemasonry in Scotland and the Founding of Grand Lodge", *Trans. Manchester Assoc. for Masonic Research*, xxvi (1936).

[3] M. Livingstone, *Guide to the Public Records of Scotland*, xiv, xv.

[4] These are listed in Livingstone, 36–7. Some lengthy extracts are given in Mylne, and shorter ones in M. and R.

[5] Extracts from Scottish state papers, made by C. N. McIntyre North, are printed in *A.Q.C.*, vii, under the title "Random Courses of Scottish Masonry". Texts of legislation relating to masons will be found in *Acts of Parliament of Scotland*, and in the *Ancient Laws and Customs of the Burghs of Scotland*, vol. ii (1424–1707).

relatively plentiful;[1] but, unfortunately, either fabric rolls have not survived, or editors have not been sufficiently interested to print them, and the student thus has little to compare with the Sacrist Rolls of Ely, or the building accounts of Westminster, Durham, York Minster or Wells. The accounts for the repairs of St. Salvator's College, St. Andrews, in 1683–90 have been printed,[2] as well as a study of the accounts for the building of the Parliament House, Edinburgh, 1632–40,[3] and we have been able to examine the unpublished accounts for the building of the Tron Kirk, Edinburgh. These are indeed useful, but they do not compensate for the absence of accounts for the building of abbeys such as Jedburgh or Melrose.

Records relating to private building are very scarce, as might be expected. Private persons were less likely than public authorities to preserve their building accounts, and, in any event, it is probable that a good deal of private building was done without detailed accounts being drawn up. Where, instead of employing the "direct labour system", a nobleman, or other considerable proprietor, had the work done for him by one or more contractors, only the day books or similar memoranda would contain the information we desire, and it is by no means impossible, or even unlikely, that many contractors conducted their businesses without such aids. To some extent, the lack of sources of this kind is compensated for by a fair number of masons' contracts, of which several are printed in Mylne, in Macgibbon and Ross, and in the publications of the various Scottish Historical Clubs.[4]

Municipal records, thanks to the activities of the Scottish Burgh Records Society, of the Historical Clubs, and, in

[1] Dr. G. G. Coulton has drawn largely on printed monastic records for his *Scottish Abbeys and Social Life*. We have seen printed cartularies, rentals, registers, and the like, relating to Arbroath, Cambuskenneth, Dunfermline, Dryburgh, Kelso, Melrose, Paisley, St. Andrews and Cupar-Angus; but with the exception of the *Rental Book of Cupar-Angus*, these sources contain very little of interest in connection with our present inquiry.

[2] See Fleming. [3] See H. and W.

[4] See *A Catalogue of the Publications of Scottish Historical and Kindred Clubs and Societies*, vol. i (1780–1908), edited by C. S. Terry; vol. ii (1908–27), edited by C. Matheson.

certain cases, of the municipalities concerned, have been made available in print in considerable numbers. Lodge records, which in two cases go back to the end of the sixteenth century, are only readily available in so far as they are quoted in the various lodge histories. In several cases, the Minute Books contain entries of much more than local interest. Thus, for example, the Schaw Statutes of 1598 are written in a minute book of the Lodge of Edinburgh, and the Falkland Statutes of 1636 in a minute book of Aitchison's Haven Lodge.

Our information about the building industry in mediaeval Scotland is too slight to enable us to trace the transition to conditions as they were in the sixteenth and seventeenth centuries. Incidentally, and by way of illustration, we have something to say about the earlier epoch; but our purpose is chiefly to describe the industry in early modern times, under five main headings: (1) the employers; (2) the organisation of building operations; (3) the administration of building operations; (4) masons' working conditions; (5) organisation among masons. In connection with various points, we draw attention, mostly in footnotes, to the similarities or contrasts afforded by English conditions;[1] in our final section, we endeavour to sum up the main differences underlying building conditions in the two countries.

1. THE EMPLOYERS

As in England, so in Scotland, the four main employers in the industry were the Crown, the Church, the municipalities, and the nobility and landed gentry.

(i) In early days, the Crown was mainly interested in the erection and repair of castles for military purposes, though in the sixteenth and seventeenth centuries it spent considerable sums on palaces and other residences. The King also appears to have made some contributions towards the

[1] To save space, we seldom give references relating to particular English conditions: we have collected together a group of references to the English Mason in a footnote to our final section, p. 72 below.

wages of masons employed at certain churches,[1] but there is no trace amongst the surviving accounts of sums in any way comparable with the vast expenditure of English kings at Westminster Abbey, or at Vale Royal Abbey. Nor have we discovered any accounts in respect of the erection of colleges at the royal expense, corresponding to Henry VI's activities at King's College, Cambridge, and at Eton College. Royal building must naturally have been limited by the smaller resources at the command of the Crown in Scotland.

(ii) The Church was mainly concerned with monastic building. Large urban churches, such as St. Giles, Edinburgh,[2] the Tron Church, Edinburgh, Our Lady Church at Dundee [3] and St. Nicholas at Aberdeen,[4] appear, at any rate in the period for which we have information, to have been the responsibility of the respective municipalities. The Church, on occasion, financed the erection of stone bridges. The undertakings of the Bishop of Dunkeld at Dunkeld in 1510–16,[5] and of the Bishop of Aberdeen at Aberdeen in 1489,[6] are comparable with that of the Archbishop of Canterbury and the Abbot of Westminster in paying for the rebuilding of the bridge over the Brent at Hanwell in 1530.[7]

(iii) The municipalities, in addition to assuming responsibility for the building and maintenance of churches, erected markets, prisons and other buildings required for administrative purposes, and on occasion, bridges.[8]

[1] The King's gift of £26 13s. 4d. for the maintenance of two masons for the fabric of the Church at St. Andrews is recorded in 1381, and a similar payment in 1384 (*Exch. R.*, iii, 70, 674).

[2] A contract dated November, 1387, between the provost and community of Edinburgh, and three master masons, for the erection of five vaulted chapels on the south side of St. Giles, is printed in *The Register of the Charters of St. Giles, Edinburgh*, 24. The work, for which the masons were to receive 600 marks sterling, was to be done in the style of St. Stephen's Chapel, Holyrood.

[3] Mylne, 63.   [4] *Aberdeen*, i, 41, 42.
[5] Account printed in Mylne, 18 *folg*.   [6] Mylne, 36, 37.
[7] *London and Midd. Arch. Soc.*, N.S., v (1928), 449 *folg*.
[8] At Aberdeen the municipality was responsible for the repair of the bridge erected by the Bishop (*Aberdeen*, i, 38–9). The bridge across the Tay at Perth was rebuilt by the municipality early in the seventeenth century with some financial assistance from the Crown (Mylne, 89 *folg*.). The burgh

(iv) The nobility and landed gentry erected castles and houses for defensive or residential purposes; as the nobility was relatively much stronger, and the Crown relatively much weaker, than in England, private castle building for defensive purposes flourished more widely, and at later dates, in Scotland than in England. Many of the houses, too, were constructed with an eye to defence, as a study of the many illustrations and plans in Macgibbon and Ross clearly shows. It must not be assumed, however, that a castle was in every case a stone structure: earthwork castles, or *mottes*, were by no means uncommon. Thus a map of the early routes from Mar to Moray, prepared to illustrate Dr. Simpson's paper on the quarry of Kildrummy,[1] shows seven stone castles and five *mottes* in an area about 20 miles square; a map printed by Dr. Mackenzie [2] shows fifty-nine *mottes* in Galloway and Dumfriesshire. The *motte*, or earliest type of castle, was a timber stronghold, and the same material continued in use for a long time. "Down to the War of Independence", writes Dr. Mackenzie, "most of the Scottish gentry were housed in castles of timber, and a steadily decreasing number of them through more than a century thereafter".[3] The use of stone probably commenced in the late thirteenth century; the first stone wall at Stirling Castle was in course of erection in 1288,[4] and from the end of the fourteenth century onwards the *motte* and bailey plan was abandoned in new structures.[5] The timber castles, or timber structures with part of the work in stone, disappeared during the fifteenth century; and during that century, an active period in castle and church building, "a castle was taking normally the character of a building or buildings in stone and lime."[6] The nobility, in addition to erecting castles and houses, were also at times responsible for other types of building; Lord Scone had a church rebuilt at

of Inverness, which erected a stone bridge in 1680–3, had considerable difficulties with the master masons (*Inverness*, ii, 284, 286, 306, 309, 317, 320, 321, 331).

[1] W. Douglas Simpson, "Lapicidarium de Kyndromy", *Aberdeen University Review*, July, 1937.

[2] W. Mackay Mackenzie, *The Mediaeval Castle in Scotland* (Rhind Lectures, 1925–6), 14.

[3] *Ibid.*, 31.   [4] *Ibid.*, 38.   [5] *Ibid.*, 72.   [6] *Ibid.*, 138.

Falkland in 1620.[1]   In an earlier period, the nobility erected collegiate churches, as the St. Clair family, for instance, built the church of Roslin.[2]

2. THE ORGANISATION OF BUILDING OPERATIONS

In Scotland, as in England, two main systems of conducting building operations can be traced: (i) what we should now call the "direct labour system," under which the employer, commonly the Crown or the Church, appointed certain officials, such as a master mason and a master of the works, to organise and administer the building operations, to arrange for supplies of materials, and to engage the necessary craftsmen and labourers; (ii) the contract system, under which either the whole or part of a building operation was let out by task or bargain to one or more tradesmen.   In England, the former system apparently applied to all larger and to many smaller works undertaken during the Middle Ages, though the contract system was by no means unknown in the thirteenth and early fourteenth centuries.   After the Black Death, the use of the direct labour system tended to decline and that of the contract system to extend, until by the end of the seventeenth century the latter system was almost universally adopted in England.

From the limited information available, it would appear that the direct labour system was relatively less important, and the contract system relatively more important, in Scotland than in England.   If original monastic and castle building accounts were available, instead of what are mostly extracts from comparatively small maintenance or repair accounts, our conclusion might possibly be different; certainly in England it was the larger operations which were the strongholds of the direct labour system.   Actually, for the thirteenth and fourteenth centuries, we can trace the direct labour system in operation in Scotland, with certainty, at Stirling Castle in 1288,[3] in 1336,[4] in 1362 [5] and in 1376–77,[6]

[1] Mylne, 110. [2] Mackenzie, *op. cit.*, 137.
[3] *Exch. R.*, i, 40. [4] *Cal. Doc. Scot.*, iii, 364 *folg.*
[5] *Exch. R.*, ii, 85. [6] *Ibid.*, ii, 524, 551.

and at Edinburgh Castle in 1335–37;[1] very possibly it was in use in 1264–6 at the repairs of Aberdeen, Dumfries and Wigtown Castles.[2]   On the other hand, at Tarbert Castle in 1326 [3] and at Berwick Castle and town wall in 1330 [4] and 1331,[5] work appears to have been done by contract.   Similarly in 1387, the provost and community of Edinburgh contracted with three master masons to enlarge the parish church of St. Giles.[6]   For the fifteenth century, we have very little information; in the second quarter, substantial work was done at Linlithgow Palace on the direct labour system,[7] whilst at the same period Druminnor Castle was erected by contract.[8]   In 1460–3, Ravenscraig Castle, on the Fifeshire coast between Kirkcaldy and Dysart, was erected by the Crown on the direct labour system.[9]

The various cases of life, long-term, and annual appointments of masons by the Abbey of Cupar-Angus, and by the municipalities of Aberdeen, Edinburgh and Dundee, in the late fifteenth and early sixteenth centuries,[10] clearly point to the direct labour system, which is well illustrated by the Dunkeld Bridge Account, 1510–16.   Commencing in 1529, the volumes of Master of Works Accounts, preserved in the Edinburgh Register House, provide numerous examples of the use of the direct labour system by the Crown in the sixteenth and seventeenth centuries. Various extracts printed in Mylne,[11] from an Account

---

[1] *Cal. Doc. Scot.*, iii, 347 *folg.*

[2] *Ibid.*, iii, 12, 27, 31.   In each of these cases a small lump sum (20 marks, £20, and 40 marks) was paid to the master mason, but there is no indication whether the work was to be done by contract or by direct labour.   As there is no reference to an indenture or agreement, we are disposed to think that the direct labour system was to be employed.

[3] *Ibid.*, iii, 53.   [4] *Ibid.*, iii, 320.   [5] *Ibid.*, iii, 397–8.

[6] *Register of the Charters of St. Giles, Edinburgh, 1344–1567*, 24.

[7] *Exch. R.*, iv. 485–6, 556.   Soon after the return of James I from England in 1424, the palace and other buildings at Linlithgow were consumed by fire, and the King at once set himself to rebuild the palace (*ibid.*, iv, pp. cxxxvi–cxxxvii).

[8] Tayler, *The House of Forbes*, 37.

[9] W. D. Simpson, *Ravenscraig Castle* (Aberdeen University Studies, 1938), 5, 6, based on the building accounts engrossed in the Exchequer Rolls.

[10] See the section on Masons, p. 32 below.   [11] Pp. 195–202.

Book of Sir William Bruce, General Surveyor of H.M. Works, relating to the repair of several palaces in Scotland about 1674 and 1675, show, however, that by the later part of the seventeenth century some at least of the mason-work was done by contract.   The erection of the Tron Church, Edinburgh, in 1635–8,[1] and of the Parliament House, Edinburgh, 1632–40,[2] are relatively late examples of important municipal works undertaken on the direct labour system.   In many more cases, however, surviving accounts show that during the sixteenth and seventeenth centuries much mason work was given out by task, and numerous surviving masons' contracts, in summarised or complete form, bear witness to the wide use of the contract system.   In so far as our information comes from building accounts, we usually learn only that certain sums were paid in part or full payment for specified tasks.[3]   Occasionally, an account tells us rather more, as for example, that several mason-contractors were employed on the same building operation,[4] or that a mason-contractor was paid partly in

---

[1] The body of the Tron Kirk was, however, finished by contract. The council decided in 1642 to agree with John Mylne to do the work for £400 sterling, "the council always finding stone, lime and scaffolding and all other necessaries except workmen and workmanship" (*Edinburgh, 1642–5*, 20). In 1643 an agreement was made with the same man to raise the steeple by thirty feet for £2,000.   Mylne was to be allowed Master of Work's wages for his task (*ibid.*, 40).

[2] See H. and W., which is based on the building account.

[3] E.g., sums of £26 13s. 4d., £66 13s. 4d., £13, £27 7s. 0d. and £10, were paid during the winter of 1504–5 to various masons in part payment for work at Stirling, Lochmabane and Holyroodhouse (*Treas. A/cs.*, ii, 275, 278, 279, 280); sums of £120 and £30 in 1512–13 to Geo. Ellis, mason, in part payment of £200 for building Our Lady Kirk of Steile (*ibid.*, iv, 283, 446); a sum of £130 14s. 4d. in 1511–12 to John Lokkert, mason, in complete payment for certain works in Stirling Castle (*ibid.*, iv, 281); and a sum of £200 in 1512 to Wm. Thome, mason, in full payment for building the hall at Falkland (*Exch. R.*, xiii, 431).   Hugh Miller, the mason-contractor for the Quay at Ayr, received payment for his task in many instalments during 1600 and 1601 (*Ayr*, 46–51).

[4] At the repair of the College, Church and Steeple of St. Andrews, 1683–90, five different mason-contractors, or firms of mason-contractors, were employed during a period of six years (Fleming), though not more than two were employed in any one year.

kind.[1] Where building operations were undertaken away from the towns, payments to mason-contractors partly in kind were probably not uncommon, and we have noted four contracts of this type at Cawdor in 1639, 1682, 1684 and 1699,[2] and one at Glamis about 1685.[3]

The various contracts we have examined show considerable differences in the methods of calculating the payments to be made by the proprietors: (i) payment of a fixed sum of money for the task,[4] or a fixed sum of money *plus* a fixed amount of food,[5] which appears to have been the commonest method; (ii) payment of a fixed sum for the task, *plus* a bounty at the discretion of the proprietor;[6] (iii) payment of a fixed sum, either of money, or of money *plus* food, for each unit of work done;[7] (iv) payment to consist of the profits of certain mills for a period of years;[8] (v) the proprietor to pay day wages, at stipulated rates, to the mason-contractor and his workmen.[9] In practically all contracts, provision was made for payment by instalments.

Of the undertakings entered into by mason-contractors, four types can be distinguished: (i) contracts where the mason-contractor undertook to find only the workmanship, the proprietor to provide all materials, including carriage,

[1] At the repair of Doune Castle in 1581, the master mason, for his contract in respect of certain works, received £100 in silver, together with 4 bolls of malt and 4 bolls of meal, worth £36 6s. 8d. (Account printed in Mylne, 60.)

[2] *Cawdor*, 283, 360, 369, 391. In the first case, where the masons were to receive 600 marks and 5 chalders of victuals, half meal and half barley, the "Discharge" (*ibid.*, 296) shows that the victuals were worth £500, as compared with £400 paid in cash.

[3] Strathmore, 64.

[4] E.g., contracts at Edinburgh in 1387 (*Charters of St. Giles*, 24) and 1578 (*Edinburgh, 1573–89*, 74–5); at Aberdeen in 1610 and 1616 (*Aberdeen*, ii, 299, 338); at Holyroodhouse in 1672 and 1676 (Mylne, 176–81, 191, 193); at Kelburn Castle in 1692 (M. and R., iv, 30).

[5] *Cawdor*, 283, 369, 391.

[6] See contract of 1589 for enlargement of Thomas Bannatyne's house (Mylne, 66–8).

[7] *Cawdor*, 360.

[8] *Charters and Documents relating to the Burgh of Peebles, 1165–1710*, 312–17.

[9] See contract for erecting tower of Old Booth, Edinburgh, in 1501 (*Edinburgh, 1403–1528*, 89–90), and Panmure House contract, 1666.

and all tackle and plant;[1] (ii) contracts where the mason-contractor undertook to win the stones and furnish the labour, the proprietor finding all other materials, also carriage, and all tackle and plant;[2] (iii) contracts where the mason-contractor, in addition to finding the labour, was to furnish stone and lime (presumably including carriage)[3] or was to win and carry stone and to burn lime,[4] the proprietor in each case to provide the other materials, and all tackle and plant; (iv) contracts where the mason-contractor was to furnish all materials (presumably including carriage), plant and tackle, and to supply all workmanship.[5] This last type of agreement clearly implies that the mason-contractor was a man of some substance; thus it was probably a relatively late development; in any case, apart from a walling contract of 1567, we have found no example of it before 1668. In three cases of this type which we have noted, Robert Mylne, the King's Master Mason, was the contractor. As he, like the English mason-contractor of this period, found it very hard to collect the sums due to him from the Crown,[6] his need for capital was even greater than the form of contract, of itself, would suggest.

Reviewing the various contracts from the point of view of the undertakings entered into by the mason-contractors,

[1] We have noted examples at Edinburgh in 1387 (*Charters of St. Giles* 24), at Aberdeen in 1532 (*Aberdeen*, i, 146), at Bannatyne's house in 1589 (Mylne 66–7), at Partick Castle in 1611 (M. and R., v, 5), and at Panmure House in 1666.

[2] Cases occur at Aberdeen in 1610 (*Aberdeen*, ii, 299), at Cawdor in 1684 and 1699 (*Cawdor*, 367–9, 391–4) and at Kelburn Castle in 1692 (M. and R., iv, 30–1). At the erection of Falkland Church in 1620, the contractor was to supply all materials and workmanship, and the parishioners were to supply carriage (Mylne, 110–11). Plant is not mentioned.

[3] As at Aberdeen in 1616 (*Aberdeen*, ii, 338 *folg.*).

[4] As at Cawdor in 1639 (*Cawdor*, 283–5).

[5] Probably the case in a Perth contract of 1668 (Mylne, 214–15), and an Edinburgh contract of 1674 (*ibid.*, 218–19); and certainly the case in a Holyroodhouse contract of 1672 (*ibid.*, 176–81). It was also the case in an Edinburgh contract of 1567, by which two masons undertook to build a town wall 6 feet thick and 7 ells high, the masons to provide sand, lime, stones, workmen, scaffolding, and all other necessaries (*Edinburgh, 1557–71*, 239).

[6] The subject of postponed payments to masons is referred to more fully below, p. 18.

we cannot help being struck by the stipulation in nearly all, that the proprietors were to supply the tackle and plant, such as scaffolding, centerings, barrows and buckets. This suggests that the tradesmen were less regularly in the contracting business than the corresponding masons in England, where, to our knowledge, this particular stipulation seldom occurs in masons' contracts. On the other hand, less stress seemed to be laid on the provision of carriage in Scottish contracts, which suggests that the quarry was in many cases much closer to the building site than in England.[1]

In most of the contracts we have examined, there appear to be no provisions regarding failure on the part of the mason-contractors, or of the proprietors, to fulfil their respective engagements. In an Aberdeen contract of 1616,[2] however, the mason had to find four sureties, and provision was made for valuing his work if he died before it was completed. In the Holyroodhouse contract of 1672,[3] Robert Mylne had to undertake to pay £200 in the event of failure to fulfil his covenants. In the Panmure House contract of 1666, and in the Cawdor contract of 1699,[4] it was provided that the proprietors were to be responsible for the workmen's wages at stipulated rates, if they were idle through the failure of the proprietors to provide materials, carriage, or plant for which they were responsible.

The Supply of Stone.—The subject of quarries, the main source of supply, is discussed below in connection with quarriers, in the section on Workers in Stone, and also in our final section. It is thus only necessary to refer here to the practice of using dressed and undressed stone from old buildings. In England, the practice can be traced to some extent in the Middle Ages, and on a large scale after the dissolution of the monasteries. In Scotland, we have no information for the Middle Ages, and only one example

[1] That the cost of carriage might be quite a serious item in Scotland is shown by the fact that at the erection of the Parliament House, Edinburgh, in 1632, the carter received 12s. in respect of carriage of stone costing 6s. 8d. to quarry (H. and W., 22). At St. Andrews in 1683, the cost of carriage of stone was equal to the purchase price at the quarry (Fleming, 237, 238). The distance in each case was 3 or 4 miles.

[2] *Aberdeen*, ii, 338 *folg.*　　　　　　　　　　　　　　[3] Mylne, 176 *folg.*
[4] *Cawdor*, 391–4.

before the seventeenth century, viz., the case of the burgh of Edinburgh, which in 1581 entered into negotiations with a man in Queen's Ferry for the purchase of ashlar and "thak staynis" of the Abbey in St. Colmes Inch for the town's work.[1] Our other references are relatively late. In 1681 the burgh of Inverness bought the Kirk of the Citadel in order that its stones might be used for the bridge then in process of erection.[2] At the repair of the College build-ings at St. Andrews in 1683–90, the College, in addition to purchasing stone from quarries, bought the stones of an old house and also paid for digging 100 cartloads of stone out of the Castle walls.[3] In the Cawdor building contract of 1699, it was provided that the mason-contractors should cast down the little tower, preserving the stones, especially the hewn work, as whole as they could, so that the old stones might be used to build the new work.[4] At Aberdeen in 1702, the Session accepted an offer of the College to purchase stones lying in the church yard for the repair of the College buildings, but whether the College obtained the stones is not clear; three months later action was taken against the master of the hospital for taking a great number of the best and finest stones lying in the church yard to rebuild the back wall and stairs of the hospital, without the consent or advice of the Session.[5]

3. THE ADMINISTRATION OF BUILDING OPERATIONS

Master Mason.—This term was used in Scotland in two entirely different senses: first, as in England, to describe the chief technical official, where the work was being done by direct labour; and secondly, to denote a master tradesman working, either as a contractor or as a salaried employee, along with his servants. In this case there might be several master masons on the same building operation.

(i) Various examples of the term "master mason" in the first sense occur in Scottish building accounts. Thus at Edinburgh Castle in 1335, we find "Master John de Kil-

---

[1] *Edinburgh, 1573–89,* 204   [2] *Inverness,* ii, 290, 295.
[3] Fleming, 238, 239.   [4] *Cawdor,* 391.
[5] *Records of Old Aberdeen,* ii, 108–10.

bourne, *cementarius*",[1] with a remuneration of 12*d*. sterling per day, for seven days a week. Later in the same account he is referred to as master mason; an entry in December 1336 shows that he was employed at Bothwell Castle at the same period.[2] Two hundred years later, in the Accounts relating to Holyroodhouse for 1529–30, John Aitone, mason, is described as "master mason," and his name appears at the head of the weekly wage-list of masons.[3] He is doubtless the same as John Aittoun, "master mason to the King's grace," who was in receipt of a yearly "pension" of £20 in 1526;[4] and as John Aytoun, master mason, who received livery clothes at the King's command in 1530.[5] The term master mason also occurs in this sense in connection with church and municipal works. Thus at Edinburgh in 1491, the burgh made a "statute anent the government of the master mason of St. Giles".[6] At Perth, at the beginning of the sixteenth century, the chief technical official at the Tay Bridge was Thomas Fothringham, mason, described in 1502 as "Master of the Fabric of Tay Bridge", and in 1508 as master mason (*principalis lathomus*).[7] In the municipal accounts relating to the building of the Tron Kirk, Edinburgh, 1635–8, John Mylne was "Mr. Mayssoun" at £6 a week, the usual wage of the masons being £3 12s. 0d. At the erection of the Parliament House, Edinburgh, another municipal enterprise, in 1632–40, John Ritchie was master mason at a weekly wage of £6, in addition to an annual retaining fee of £100.[8]

Among the master masons employed by the Crown, some are described as King's Master Masons. Mylne, in his *Master Masons to the Crown of Scotland*, interprets the term rather narrowly, and restricts his study to those appointed under the privy seal. Of these, he lists nine in the

---

[1] *Cal. Doc. Scot.*, iii, 347 *folg*. As this is an English document, the presumption is that payments were in terms of pounds sterling and not of pounds Scots.

[2] His position appears to have been very similar to that of Nicholas de Derneford, who was appointed master mason at Beaumaris Castle in 1316, and was later responsible for all the King's castles in North Wales (*Cal. Pat. R., 1313–17*, 457; *1321–4*, 353).

[3] M.o.W. A/cs., i.   [4] *Treas. A/cs.*, v, 268.
[5] *Ibid.*, v, 431.   [6] *Edinburgh, 1403–1528*, 61, 62.
[7] *Exch. R.*, xii, 99; xiii, 241.   [8] H. and W., 25.

sixteenth and seventeenth centuries, commencing with John Brownhill, appointed in 1532.[1] The term can, however, fairly be interpreted more widely, so as to include not only the previously mentioned John Aittoun, "master mason to the King's grace", but others who, like Aittoun, received a yearly "pension" or retaining fee from the Crown, and possibly a livery. In this category we place Nicholas de Hane, described in 1402 as King's mason (*simentarius regis*),[2] who was doubtless the same as Master Nicholas, "King's Keybearer and Mason". The latter in 1401, for service and labour, was granted, during life, an annuity of £10, charged on the customs of Dundee.[3] We are unable to say exactly what his services were, but in 1377-9 he was engaged in making a tomb for Robert II, for which he was to receive £120.[4] Similarly, we include John Lokkert, described in 1508 as "our servant and mason" in a letter under the great seal granting him a "pension" of £20, charged on the customs of Ayr, "for good, gratuitous and faithful service to us."[5] The "pension", which was subject to his remaining in the royal service, was clearly stated to be in addition to his wages. In 1511, he was supplied with a "livery without bonnet".[6] He can be traced at Stirling Castle in various years between 1504 and 1513.[7] In the latter year he was one of several masons who, with their servants, were paid £10 to pass to England.[8] Another mason who probably enjoyed the status of King's Master Mason, though we cannot trace a document in which he is so described, was Walter Merlioun, to whom a "pension" of £40, charged on the customs of Edinburgh, was granted in 1499.[9]

[1] The other eight are Thomas Franche, appointed 1535; Mogin Martyn, Frenchman, 1536; Nicholas Roy, Frenchman, 1539; John Roytell, Frenchman, 1557; William Wallace, 1617; John Mylne, elder, 1631; John Mylne, younger, 1636; Robert Mylne, 1668.

[2] *Exch. R.*, iii, 562. [3] *Ibid.*, iii, 536. [4] *Ibid.*, ii, 585, 622.

[5] *Ibid.*, xiii, 360. [6] *Treas. A/cs.*, iv, 258.

[7] *Ibid.*, ii, 275, 281; iv, 44, 281, 372, 527.

[8] *Ibid.*, iv, 520. See also the section on Recruitment, p. 47 below.

[9] Grant printed in Mylne, 10. We know that the pension was paid in 1504 and 1507 (*Treas. A/cs.*, ii, 339; iv, 69), and that he worked at Stirling in 1496 (M. and R., v, 529) and at Holyroodhouse in 1502 (*Treas. A/cs.*, ii, 344, and M. and R., v, 530). We cannot trace any grant of a livery.

Without making any special effort to trace the history of the later King's Master Masons, we have noted one or two points concerning them. Thus, the fee of John Roitell, the King's French Master Mason, was £50 per annum;[1] in the case of John Brownhill, we have noted that he received, in 1539, his fee of £20 in respect of 1537,[2] and that, in 1540, he received £32 6s. od. for his "bounteth" (bounty, fee), "and to buy him clothes because he got never none of them before".[3] The delay in paying the fees and providing the clothes of King's Master Masons appears to have become gradually worse. An abstract of accounts, prepared by Robert Mylne,[4] shows that in 1681 his salary in respect of 1677, 1678, 1679 and 1680 was still owing to him, and a petition of 1708 [5] states that his fee of £10 sterling per annum, and a further sum of £10 sterling per annum in lieu of a suit of clothes, was due to him for the twenty years from Martinmas 1688 to Martinmas 1708. Even larger sums were due to Robert Mylne in respect of Crown contracts. In 1699 a sum of £1818 sterling was owing to him in respect of work done at Holyroodhouse at various dates commencing 1676, and a sum of £362 sterling for contracts at Edinburgh Castle between 1677 and 1685.[6] In 1699, he assigned his claim for £10 sterling, in respect of work done at Holyroodhouse in 1689, to a writer to the signet "for a certain sum of money presently advanced and paid to me".[7]

King's Master Masons were not the only master masons to experience difficulty in obtaining payment. In March 1639–40, John Mylne, master mason at the building of Tron Kirk, Edinburgh, received a sum of £188 6s. in part payment of his weekly wage (£6) due to him, which shows that his wages were more than 30 weeks in arrears.[8] In

[1] *Treas. A/cs.*, x, 355; xi, 67, 88, 167, 220, 434, 514.
[2] *Ibid.*, vii, 160.   [3] *Ibid.*, vii, 415.   [4] Printed in Mylne, 233.
[5] Printed in Mylne, 235.   [6] Mylne, 233.
[7] Deed of Assignment printed in Mylne, 234.
[8] Payments due to English master masons and mason-contractors were also sometimes in arrears. For examples relating to the thirteenth and fourteenth centuries, see our *Mediaeval Mason*, 5 n.; for examples relating to the seventeenth and early eighteenth centuries, see *ibid.*, 194 and our *London Mason in the Seventeenth Century*, 37, 50, 51.

June 1642 the town owed him £873 13s. 4d. for his "pension" since 1637, and there were arrears owing to him in December 1646. In 1652 the municipality owed him 1,200 marks on account of St. Giles steeple and 5,880 marks on account of stone work in the fortifications of Leith.[1]

The relation of the master mason to planning and designing is discussed in a later section. Apart from that, the exact duties of a master mason are nowhere exactly defined. In some cases, he was probably little more than a foreman and superior craftsman, working with his own hands with the general body of masons;[2] in other cases, he was rather a consultant or supervisor, who was not necessarily present at the building operation all the time. That this was so in the case of Master John de Kilbourne, who was responsible for more than one royal castle simultaneously in the fourteenth century, has already been indicated. It was also true of John Brown, master of the masons at Dunkeld Bridge in 1513, for the Building Account shows that he was paid twelve marks a year to attend at the work four times a year, for two weeks on each occasion. John Mylne, master mason at the erection of Panmure House in 1666, held a similar position. According to the building contract, he undertook to be present at the foundation, when everything could be discussed, and at the beginning of every story, as the building advanced in height. Earlier in the contract, Mylne undertook to provide "a sufficient qualified able mason", an agent afterwards referred to as the master overseer, to have the charge and direction of the masons. Mylne's overseer was to receive £6 13s. 4d. a week, compared with £5 6s. 8d. paid to senior masons.

(ii) The use of the term "master mason" in the sense of master tradesman is clearly brought out in a resolution of the Town Council of Linlithgow in July 1668, by which the dean of gild and baillies were ordered "to concord

---

[1] *Edinburgh, 1642–45*, 10, 106, 293.

[2] According to the terms of William Aytoun's appointment as master mason at Heriot's Hospital, Edinburgh, in 1632, he was to mould and carve, and to direct the other masons to hew, mould and carve (Mylne, 116; cf. also M. and R., v, 540).

and settle with a Master Mason for the building of our Tolbooth".[1]   The same meaning must obviously be attached to the expression where several "master masons" were paid in connection with the same operation.   Thus, at Edinburgh in 1517, payment was made to six master masons "hewing . . . taking down and remaking a chimney".[2]   At Holyroodhouse in 1535–6, John Brownhill, master mason, and Andrew Vilertoun, master mason of Perth, the former at 18s. a week, the latter at 16s. a week, were employed at the same time, each accompanied by a number of masons.[3] At the rebuilding of the Edinburgh city cross in 1617, six master masons at £4 per week, and eight other masons at £2 10s. 0d., were employed.[4]   These various master masons were employed at day or weekly wages.[5]

Master of Work.—The long series of volumes of Master of Works Accounts, preserved in the Edinburgh Register House, is a clear indication that the master of work was an administrative and financial officer, whatever other functions he might discharge.   Officials having this title were appointed by the employer—the Crown, the Church or a municipality as the case might be.[6]   In the case of Masters of Work to the Crown of Scotland, the various writs of appointment [7] throw some light upon the duties of the office.

[1] Extract quoted in Mylne, 242.   [2] *Treas. A/cs.*, v, 121.
[3] M.o.W. A/cs., iv.   [4] Treasurer's accounts printed in Mylne, 106.
[5] The use of the term "master mason", "master freestone mason", "master freemason", to denote a master tradesman, is relatively rare in England; it does occur, however, in certain statutes and wage assessments.   We know of no English case of several master tradesmen and their workmen being employed at day or weekly wages on the same building operation; the nearest analogy with which we are acquainted occurred at the rebuilding of St. Paul's Cathedral, where at one period two, at another period four, and at yet another period six, mason-contractors were engaged simultaneously, each with his own staff of masons.
[6] Quite possibly a private employer engaged in building might appoint a master of work, but we do not know of an instance.   At the repair of St. Salvator's College, St. Andrews, in 1683–90, the Provost of the College kept the accounts (Fleming).
[7] A score of these, preserved in the Registers of the Privy Seal, are transcribed in R. S. Mylne, "Masters of Work to the Crown of Scotland", *Proc. Soc. Antiq. Scot.*, 1895–6, 49–68, and it is upon these records that we base our remarks.

The officer was sometimes appointed to a particular work,[1] in other cases to all royal castles, palaces and other works in Scotland.[2] In some of the appointments, the term Principal Master of all His Majesty's Works and Buildings, or an expression to that effect, occurs.[3] By the terms of some grants, the Master of Work was given power to appoint deputies, for whom he was to be responsible;[4] in other cases, the principal or chief overseers and attenders were appointed directly by the Crown.[5] They were to work wherever directed by the Principal Master of Work; in his absence, they were to have "power and commandment of all craftsmen on our said sovereign lord's works".[6] The master of work was to superintend the appointment of workmen and to agree with them about rates and prices and other conditions; he was to render an account and reckoning to the Treasury of the agreements entered into, and of all monies received and expended by him.[7] In at least one case, he was given power to hold courts by himself or his deputies, and to punish transgressors at the works under his charge.[8] A possibility that H.M. Master of Work might be concerned in the problems of planning and designing is suggested by an entry in the accounts relating to the building of the Parliament House, Edinburgh. In February, 1633, the Town Council authorised a payment of £1,000 to Sir James Murray, H.M. Master of Work, for his past services to the town and "for drawing up ane model" of the Parliament and Session House.[9] In the writ appointing Murray to his office, which he held jointly with Anthonie Alexander, he and Alexander are referred to as "general surveyors and principal masters of all his majesty's

[1] E.g., Sir James Nycholay to Stirling Castle in 1529 (*ibid.*, 53).

[2] E.g., John Hammyltoune in 1543 and Sir Robert Drummond in 1579 (*ibid.*, 54).

[3] E.g., in the grants to Sir James Hammyltoun in 1539 (*ibid.*, 53) and to Sir Wm. Bruce in 1671 (*ibid.*, 60).

[4] E.g., Sir Robert Drummond in 1579 (*ibid.*, 54) and Sir Wm. Bruce in 1671 (*ibid.*, 60).

[5] E.g., Wm. Govane and James Murray in 1632 (*ibid.*, 58).

[6] *Ibid.*, 58, 59.   [7] *Ibid.*, 60.   [8] *Ibid.*, 61.

[9] H. and W., 18, 19.

works";[1] in the writ appointing Sir William Bruce in 1671 mention is actually made of his skill in architecture.[2] We know of three English cases in the sixteenth century of surveyors of works being responsible for plans or "plats",[3] but in at least two of these cases the men were carpenters, by origin. Whether the expression "surveyor general" must be regarded as implying some technical qualifications in the case of Murray and Alexander we do not know, but as we shall show in the next section, it was the King's Master Masons in the seventeenth century who normally supplied plans and designs when these were required, and we are disposed to think that it was quite exceptional for H.M. Masters of Work to take a professional interest in architecture.

With regard to municipal masters of work, the Aberdeen records are the most informative. In 1441, the Council decided that henceforth "two men of good cunning and knowledge" should be appointed masters of the common work of the town, and that they were to collect all town rents and to spend the proceeds as directed by the Alderman and Common Council.[4] In 1477, Alexander of Chavmyr, alderman, was continued for two years to come "upper and principal master of work" of the building of St. Nicholas choir.[5] In 1623, the master of work of the Tolbooth steeple was instructed to pay £100 to John Mylne, mason of Dundee, as part payment for free ashlar and workmanship.[6] These references all point to the master of work being a financial officer. Similarly with Robert Kidstone, baker, and Robert Stevinsone, merchant, who were appointed overseers and attenders of the bridge mill at Stirling in 1652, "for buying of timber and other furniture thereto, agreeing with and paying of the workmen, and doing of what else shall be necessary to be done, for which effect money is to be presently provided and given to them".[7] Another

---

[1] Mylne, "Masters of Work to the Crown of Scotland", 57.

[2] *Ibid.*, 60.

[3] See our *Sixteenth Century Mason*, 6, 7, for the cases of James Nedham, Lawrence Bradshaw and Henry Hawthorne.

[4] *Aberdeen*, i, 7.   [5] *Ibid.*, i, 35–6.   [6] *Ibid.*, ii, 379.

[7] *Stirling*, 206.

Aberdeen reference, however, relating to Master John Gray, mason, in 1484, gives an entirely different picture. In that year, the municipal authorities resolved that Master John Gray, mason, was to be received as Master of Work of St. Nicholas;[1] it is recorded that "he has taken upon him to be continually labouring and diligent ... and to do all care concerning the said work that accords to a master of work, both in labouring of his own person, in devising, and in supervising the masons and workmen under him. He shall labour himself and cause the workmen under him to labour daily and continually after the Act of Parliament made thereupon."[2] Here the term "master of work" is obviously used as equivalent to "master mason", a practice not unknown in England. We are disposed to think that the somewhat similar term "master of the fabric" may also have had two meanings; a payment of £100 in 1426 to "Walter Masoun, burgess of Edinburgh, master of the fabric of Edinburgh Castle",[3] suggests a financial officer, as £100 Scots, equivalent at that date to about £50 sterling, represented a very substantial sum of money. On the other hand, payments of £7 6s. 2d. and of 40s. in 1443 and 1446 to John of Peebles, mason, "master of the fabric of Tay Bridge",[4] suggest an ordinary master mason. In the early sixteenth century, Thomas Fothringham, mason, described on several occasions as "Master of the Fabric of Tay Bridge",[5] is later described as "master mason".[6]

Two other sets of municipal records in which we have noted references to "masters of work" are those of Edinburgh in 1536 and 1555-6,[7] and Lanark in the late seventeenth century,[8] but such appointments were very common. The only abbey in which we have been able to trace such an official is Cupar-Angus in the late fifteenth century.[9] At St. Andrews there was a "Master of the

---

[1] *Aberdeen*, i, 41.

[2] Presumably the Act of 1469 regarding work on Saturdays and eves of festivals (*Laws*, 33), discussed on p. 41 below.

[3] *Exch. R.*, iv, 410.   [4] *Ibid.*, v, 142, 245.

[5] *Ibid.*, xii, 99, 173, 276, 385, 477, 602.

[6] *Ibid.*, xiii, 109, 241, 380, 397, 498, 583.

[7] *Edinburgh*, 1528-57, 74, 324.   [8] *Lanark*, 146, 237, 380.

[9] *Cupar*, i, 309; ii, 173, 208.

Kyrk werk" responsible for the fabric of the parish church as early as 1503.[1] In all these cases the evidence suggests that the functions of the official were administrative rather than technical.

Plans and Designs.—In Scotland, as in England, bishops and abbots did much to further certain building operations, but there, as elsewhere, it would be a mistake to regard them as the architects of the churches, bridges, or monastic houses with which they were connected.[2] Masons appear to have been the mediaeval architects and to have prepared such plans and designs as were used.[3] In England, we find an increasing reference to plans or "plats" in the sixteenth century, and also indications that some of them were prepared by persons other than masons.[4] The corresponding development in Scotland cannot, so far as we are aware, be traced until the seventeenth century, when we find not only some indication of the appearance of the professional architect, but also a tendency for the nobility and gentry to take a practical interest in planning and designing. Nevertheless, the available evidence shows that, even in the seventeenth century, the mason-architect was still a very important factor in the Scottish building industry.

In the previous section, we noted that in 1484 "devising" was specified amongst the duties of Master John Gray, mason, at St. Nicholas, Aberdeen; we have little doubt that the term was used in the sense of designing or planning, as in English documents of the fourteenth and sixteenth centuries. Whether the term was used in the same sense in 1497, when the master mason at Linlithgow rode to Stirling Castle to "gif his devis to the work",[5] is not clear; very possibly he was called upon only for advice. That a mason might be consulted is clearly shown by two entries in the Dunkeld Bridge Accounts for 1513 and 1514.

---

[1] *Statutes of the Scottish Church, 1225–1559,* 119 n.

[2] See A. H. Thompson, "Mediaeval building accounts and what we learn from them", *Trans. Somerset Arch. Soc.,* 1920; reprinted in *Misc. Lat.,* 1927–8.

[3] See our "Decline of the Mason-Architect in England", *R.I.B.A. Journal,* Sept., 1937; and our *Introduction to Freemasonry,* 25 *folg.*

[4] See our *Sixteenth Century Mason,* 5 *folg.*

[5] M. and R., v, 530.

On the first occasion, a sum of 10s. was paid to Thomas Fothringham "coming to Dunkeld to visit the work of the bridge and for his advice about the work". On the second occasion, a sum of 4s. 2d. was spent on drink for Thomas Fothringham and John Cowts, masons, "coming to Dunkeld for their advice at the work". Fothringham was almost certainly the Master Mason at the Bridge of Tay at Perth;[1] Cowts was doubtless the mason of that name who had worked at Dunkeld Bridge in 1512 and 1513;[2] probably he was the John Kowtis who received a life appointment as mason of the burgh of Stirling in 1529.[3] In 1539, a sum of £5 10s. 0d. was paid to French masons coming to St. Andrews for their advice concerning the building of the new College.[4]

For the seventeenth century, we have more definite evidence of plans and designs. William Aytoun, jun., Master Mason at Heriot's Hospital, Edinburgh, 1631–43, designed Innes House, Morayshire, and was paid £26 13s. 4d. for drawing the form of the house on paper.[5] In 1636, when lodges were erected in connection with the building of the Tron Church, Edinburgh, a study, presumably to serve as a drawing office, was provided at the end of the lodge for the master mason. "The Survayes and plat" made in October 1663 by John Mylne, King's Master Mason, for a new palace at Holyrood, are preserved in the Bodleian Library.[6] In 1666, in the contract for the building of Panmure House, John Mylne undertook to erect the house according to the manner, form and dimensions of the edifice designed and set down by him in draughts. In November, 1667, the Linlithgow Town Council approved the plans of John Mylne for a new Tolbooth, three stories high, and authorised the payment to him of his expenses, amounting to £88 12s. 0d.[7] In 1671, the more ambitious scheme for a new palace having been given up, instructions were issued for plans to be prepared for substantial alterations to Holy-

---

[1] *Exch. R.*, xii, 99; xiii, 241, 583. [2] Mylne, 23.
[3] *Stirling*, 35–7. [4] *Rentale Sancti Andree*, 68.
[5] Mylne, 139, and M. and R., v, 561.
[6] Mylne, 148, where the plans are reproduced.
[7] Mylne, 240–1, where the plans are reproduced.

roodhouse, and six original drawings, executed by Robert Mylne, King's Master Mason, have survived.[1]

About the time when the Earl of Panmure was using the services of John Mylne at Panmure House, Patrick, first Earl of Strathmore, was his own architect in remodelling Glamis Castle.[2] An earlier example of an amateur acting as architect occurred in 1633, when Dr. William Gordon, Professor of Medicine at Aberdeen, designed the crown of the steeple at the college to replace one which had been blown down.[3] A possible example of a professional architect is to be found in the Records of the Burgh of Glasgow in October, 1678, when the Council gave license to Alexander Thom, "architectour", to reside in the burgh and to exercise his employment and calling in "architectorie or in measonrie".[4]

4. MASONS' WORKING CONDITIONS

Workers in Stone.—If we may judge by the building accounts and other records we have examined, there was far less differentiation among stone workers in Scotland than in England. The main classes we have been able to trace are (i) quarriers, (ii) cowans and (iii) masons. Even so, the dividing lines between the different classes are very uncertain.

(i) *Quarriers.*—At what point the functions of quarriers ceased, and those of masons began, is not clear, since some kinds of work might be performed by either category. At the repair of Doune Castle in 1581,[5] the quarrier was paid £26 13s. 4d. for winning 160 stones, and it was he, apparently, who was paid £6 for "broching" them in the quarry, "that the horse might bring them easier home".[6] A contract of 1670 between the magistrates of Linlithgow and

---

[1] Mylne, 171, where the plans are reproduced.
[2] Strathmore, 42. [3] M. and R., v, 563.
[4] *Glasgow*, 1663–90, 259. [5] Account printed in Mylne, 60.
[6] To broach is "to work with a chisel" (*O.E.D.*), but we are inclined to think that the payment in this instance was for roughdressing with an axe. "Broachaxes" (brocheaux), "broachingaxes" (brochyngaxes), occur among the quarry tools at Stapleton (Yorks.) in 1399, and at Durham in 1457–8 (see our "English Medieval Quarry", *Economic History Review*, Nov. 1938).

James Young, quarrier, provided that Young should "win, put out and square" all sorts of stones necessary for building the Tolbooth.[1] That quarriers might sell hewn work, presumably prepared by themselves, is shown by an entry of 1610, in the Glasgow records, forbidding quarriers in the future to sell, without licence, hewn work of any sort, or wall stone, to strangers.[2] In other cases the winning and dressing of stone appear to have been done by masons. Thus at Cawdor in 1639, the masons were paid "for winning of the stones, hewing thereof and building of the old hall and kitchen",[3] and in 1684 masons were paid "to win stones in the quarry at Calder for the said work".[4] At the repair of the College at St. Andrews, Thomas Coventrie, mason, was paid £475 in 1688 "for mason and quarry work wrought by him and his men".[5] According to an Edinburgh contract of 1532, certain calsay (causeway) makers, or paviors, were to "win stones in the quarry and dress them and lay them".[6] At Lanark in 1695, the dean of gild agreed with two masons for winning a thousand stones.[7] In 1548 we find two men described as "masons and quarriers" at the siege of Huntley House,[8] and four men so described in 1550.[9]

At Inverness in 1680, there is a reference to masons and quarriers working at the quarry for winning stones for the use of the bridge.[10] As it was stipulated that the master mason should leave a skilful and sufficient mason to oversee the masons working in the quarry,[11] it may well be that the masons were mainly engaged in dressing stone there. Clear examples of this are not uncommon. A contract of 1508 between John Marser, mason, and the provost and baillies of Edinburgh, provided that Marser was to be rewarded reasonably for "broching" and dressing stone at the quarry.[12] The accounts of Dunkeld Bridge for 1513 show a payment of 24s. to John Anderson, mason, "being in the quarry and cutting stones." In the Holyroodhouse accounts for 1529–30,

[1] Contract printed in Mylne, 241. [2] *Glasgow, 1573–1642*, 313–14.
[3] *Cawdor*, 296. [4] *Ibid.*, 396. [5] Fleming, 243.
[6] *Edinburgh, 1528–57*, 57–8. [7] *Lanark*, 257. [8] *Treas. A/cs.*, ix, 375.
[9] *Ibid.*, ix, 406. [10] *Inverness*, ii, 286. [11] *Ibid.*, 284.
[12] Contract printed in Mylne, 9.

there is a reference to the barrowmen serving the masons, quarriers and workmen at the quarry;[1] the presumption is that the masons were engaged in dressing the stone which the quarriers had won. In 1553–4, two masons at Edinburgh were paid for dressing a hundred stones at the quarry.[2] At the building of the Parliament House, Edinburgh, masons were sent in 1635 to the quarry at Ravelston to dress stones on the spot.[3] This quarry, near Edinburgh, had been worked at a much earlier date, having been leased for life in 1512 to Robert Cunningham, quarrier, at £3 a year and one cow's grass; Cunningham was to furnish stone to the kirk work, the residents of the town and the common works of the town.[4] The burgh was also interested in a quarry at Granton Craig, from which three quarriers in January, 1574, contracted to win 2000 stones before Whitsun, for which they were to be paid at agreed rates, the Treasurer hiring boats to bring the stones from Granton to Leith.[5] Another example of leasing a quarry occurs in 1660, when the town quarry of Glasgow was leased to John Clark for 15 years free of rent, in consideration of his expenses in opening it; he was to serve the inhabitants with stones in conformity to the quality, quantity and prices previously stipulated.[6] Further reference to the town quarries of Glasgow occurs in 1728, when the town undertook to extend a causeway to them, members of the Incorporation of Masons to pay towards the cost certain cart dues on stones loaded at the quarries. After the cost had been reimbursed, the cart dues were to be paid to the Incorporation of Masons for the maintenance of the causeway.[7]

(ii) *Cowans.*—We have noted only two building accounts in which this word occurs, namely, those for Edinburgh Castle in 1616[8] and 1626.[9] The first shows that two cowans were employed in the first week of October, 1616, and one in the following week; the second shows that two cowans were employed for two days, and one for six days, in the first week of April, 1626. On neither occasion does

---

[1] M.o.W. A/cs., i.   [2] *Edinburgh, 1528–57*, 288.   [3] H. and W., 40.
[4] *Edinburgh, 1403–1528*, 136.   [5] *Edinburgh, 1573–89*, 10, 12.
[6] *Glasgow, 1630–62*, 445.   [7] *Glasgow, 1718–38*, 299.
[8] M.o.W. A/cs., xv.   [9] Account printed in Mylne, 74.

a mason appear to have been employed in the same week. One cowan received 16s. 8d. a day, one 13s., one 12s., one 10s., and two 6s., as compared with a mason's normal rate of 12s. a day on the same building operations. The accounts, unfortunately, throw no light upon what work the cowans did.

Jamieson's *Scottish Dictionary* defines "cowan" as "one who builds dry walls, otherwise denominated a drydiker", and the O.E.D. gives a very similar meaning—"one who builds drystone walls". Such evidence as we have been able to collect from contemporary documents does not entirely support this definition. A minute of May, 1636, of the Incorporation of Wrights, Coopers and Masons of the Burgh of Canongate [1] records that John McCoull, cowan, was admitted "to work as a cowan any work with stone and clay alone, without lime"; a later minute of May, 1649,[2] records the admission of William Reull, *cowaner*,[3] "to work as a cowan any work with stone and clay alone, without lime, excepting only to cast with lime timber door cheeks and timber windows and clay chimney heads without". The minutes of the Incorporation of Masons of Glasgow for 17 February, 1623, record that John Shedden was received and booked as a cowan, and authorised "to work stone and mortar and to build mortar walls, but not above an ell in height, and without power to work or lay hewn work, or to build with sand and lime".[4] Two negative indications are provided by a minute of the Lodge of Edinburgh, of July, 1599, which states that a mason confessed that he had offended against the deacon and masters by placing a cowan to work at a chimney head,[5] and by a minute of the Glasgow Incorporation of Masons, of December, 1600, which forbade a freeman to have cowans in his company or to suffer them to work, hew windows or doors, or sell stones.[6] The Schaw Statutes of 1598 laid it down that no master or fellow of the craft should receive any cowan to work in his company, or send any of his servants to work with cowans, under penalty of £20 for each offence, a provision which

[1] Printed in Murray, 198.   [2] *Ibid.*
[3] The word *cowaner* occurs in the Canongate records at least a dozen times between 1650 and 1670 (Murray, 199).
[4] Cruikshank, 70.   [5] Lyon, 25.   [6] Cruikshank, 65.

is repeated in the Schaw Statutes of 1599. A minute of Aitchison's Haven Lodge on 7 January, 1600, records that a mason was fined £10 for having a cowan in his company,[1] and a minute of the Lodge of Edinburgh in December, 1693, forbade any master to employ a cowan under penalty of £12 for each offence.[2] These prohibitions against working with cowans suggest a secondary and wider meaning of the word, which is given by both Jamieson and the *O.E.D.*, viz., a man who does the work of a mason but has not been regularly apprenticed or bred to the trade. It was partly at least to prevent cowans from doing the work of qualified masons, that the latter were entrusted with the Mason Word as a means of proving themselves.[3] This doubtless explains why in 1707 Mother Kilwinning Lodge defined a cowan as "a mason without the word".[4]

(iii) *Masons.*—In thirteen- and fourteenth-century Scottish documents, the word commonly used to indicate mason was *cementarius*,[5] and in the fifteenth century, *lathomus*,[6] as was also the case in England. In Scotland, however, we have found no distinction between hewers and layers at this period, and the same is not infrequently true of the craftsmen described as "masons", "masounis", "mayssonis", in the sixteenth and seventeenth centuries.[7] Occasionally, as our information indicates, a distinction was made in Scotland between hewers and layers. Thus in the Holyroodhouse accounts for 1535–6,[8] there are payments to "masonis hewaris be task"; we have not noted any definite reference to layers in these accounts, but there is a payment to "masonis layand harthis and paithment". At Ayr, in 1538–9, wages were paid to "hewers of stone" at the haven.[9]

---

[1] Wallace-James, 35, 36. [2] Lyon, 25. [3] Cf. pp. 57–8 below.

[4] See *O.E.D.*, under "cowan". On the purpose and usefulness of the Mason Word, see p. 59 below.

[5] E.g., *Exch. R.*, i, 12, 40; iii, 70; *Cal. Doc. Scot.*, iii, 347, 361.

[6] E.g., *Exch. R.*, iv, 450, 485; vi, 656; vii, 79, 363, 657.

[7] In England, it was rather the exception for the words *cementarius*, *lathomus* or mason (prior to the seventeenth century) to be used in a wide sense to include all stoneworkers other than quarriers. For the many terms used to differentiate the various types of mason, see our *Mediaeval Mason*, 82–8, and our *Sixteenth Century Mason*, 10–12.

[8] M.o.W. A/cs., iv. [9] *Ayr*, 80.

In an Edinburgh contract of 1578 it was provided that the contractor was to begin "with a sufficient number of work-men, hewers, layers and barrowmen".[1] At the building of Partick Castle in 1611, the mason-contractor under-took to provide hewers, layers, and barrowmen.[2] At the erection of the Tron Church, Edinburgh, in 1638 two men were described as "leirs mayssonis" on one occasion, and as "layeris" on another. In a contract of 1567 for the building of the Edinburgh town wall,[3] the mason-con-tractors undertook to provide masons, layers, quarriers and barrowmen, so that the term "mason" was apparently used in this instance in the sense of hewer. Other special terms sometimes used in Scotland were sculptor,[4] carver,[5] and calsay maker.[6]

In view of the relatively few cases in which a distinction appears to have been drawn between mason hewers and mason layers we must assume that masons in Scotland normally did both sorts of work, even though we can seldom find explicit evidence to support our assumption. The case of masons at Cawdor who were paid in 1639 to win stones, to hew them and to build, has already been mentioned.[7]

Building accounts frequently show that Scottish masons had "servants" or "servitors",[8] but it is not always clear from the contexts what these men did. They may have been merely labourers mixing mortar and carrying mortar and stones, but we rather doubt it, as in several cases "barrowmen serving the masons" were employed on the same operations.[9] In these cases, at least, the likelihood

---

[1] *Edinburgh, 1573–89*, 74–5.

[2] Contract printed in M. and R., v, 5.   [3] *Edinburgh, 1557–71*, 239.

[4] A memorandum of land let by the Abbey of Paisley in 1460 to Thomas Hector, sculptor, is printed in J. Cameron Lees, *The Abbey of Paisley*, 166.

[5] The name of William Wallace, carver, appears first amongst the masons employed at Edinburgh Castle in Aug. 1616 (M.o.W. A/cs., xv). Early the following year he was appointed King's Master Mason.

[6] *Edinburgh, 1528–57*, 57.

[7] *Cawdor*, 296. On this point, see also the section on Gloves, p. 42 below.

[8] E.g., *Treas. A/cs.*, ii, 362; iv, 520; v, 23, 67; viii, 453.

[9] E.g., at Holyroodhouse in 1529–30 (M.o.W. A/cs., i); at Linlithgow Palace in 1534–5 (*ibid.*, iv); at Falkland Palace in 1537–8 (*ibid.*, v); at Edinburgh Castle in 1539 (*Treas. A/cs.*, vii, 218).

is that the servant or servitor was either a learner or a qualified journeyman. Where one mason had several servants, as not infrequently happened, we think that it was almost certainly a case of a master tradesman and his workmen, all probably qualified masons, who worked as journeymen for wages instead of setting up for themselves as small masters or mason-contractors.

The manuscript and printed sources which we have been able to examine are unfortunately not sufficiently detailed to enable a very adequate picture of masons' working conditions in Scotland to be drawn. Nevertheless, we have attempted, in the following sections, to sketch the main problems connected with their employment,[1] but at almost every turn we are handicapped by the want of those continuous and detailed building accounts, which are such a valuable source of information about English masons. Thus we know but little about the distinction between summer and winter rates, the extent to which church holidays were observed, or paid for, or the regularity and continuity of employment amongst masons, and practically nothing about their by-occupations,[2] or their promotion from less to more responsible posts.[3]

Occasionally masons in Scotland enjoyed life appointments; we have noted municipal appointments of this kind at Aberdeen in 1484,[4] at Stirling in 1529,[5] and at Dundee in 1536,[6] and a monastic appointment at Cupar-Angus in 1497.[7] In two cases at Cupar-Angus, in 1485 and 1492, masons were appointed for a period of five years.[8] Annual

[1] The discussion of the masons' workshop, or lodge, is deferred until the subject of the lodge is treated as a whole in connection with Organization among Masons (see p. 60 below).

[2] Two possible cases are those of Thomas Hector, sculptor, who in the second half of the fifteenth century had an agricultural holding near Paisley Abbey at a low rental on condition that the monastery had first claim on his services (J. Cameron Lees, *op. cit.*, 166), and Thomas Mason, mason, who leased the mill at Ussy early in the sixteenth century (*Exch. R.*, xii, 663).

[3] For the possible cases of John Kowtis (Cowts) and George Boiss (Boy) see pp. 25 above and 33 below.

[4] *Aberdeen*, i, 41.   [5] *Stirling*, 35-7.   [6] Indenture printed in Mylne, 63-4.
[7] *Cupar*, i, 309.   [8] *Ibid.*, i, 304, 307.

engagements of masons are recorded at Stirling in 1375,[1] at Aberdeen in 1484, 1493 and 1498,[2] and at the erection of Dunkeld Bridge in 1510–15.[3] In all these cases, the wages are given as so much per annum. The great majority of masons enjoyed no such tenure; their wages were generally stated as so much per week or so much per day, and they were doubtless subject to dismissal at short notice, as in England. In one case at Dunkeld, in 1511–12, the accounts show that George Boy, mason, was paid one firlot [of meal] "for one week on trial".[4]

In the event of illness, accident, or old age, employers appear to have assumed some responsibility. George Boiss, who was very possibly the same as the above-mentioned George Boy, held a life appointment as mason to the Kirk of Our Lady and to the Burgh of Dundee, and was entitled to his wage for forty days in the event of infirmity or sickness, and then to no more until back at work.[5] In 1617–18, the Burgh of Ayr paid £10 to a surgeon for curing a mason of a hurt sustained while working at the bridge.[6] At the erection of the Parliament House, Edinburgh, 1632–40, various payments were made in respect of sick or injured workmen, mostly to surgeons for attendance.[7] At Edinburgh Castle in 1639, a sum of £40 was paid to a surgeon for mending a workman's eyes by the space of 12 weeks.[8] The accounts of the Burgh of Ayr show that a sum of £2 was paid in poor relief to "ane pure auld failyeit masoun" in 1616–17;[9] and those of the Parliament House that four ells of linen were provided for the winding sheet of a mason who had died.[10] In 1552–3 the Crown paid 40s. to a mason in Hamilton because his purse had been stolen.[11] We have found several cases of "pensions" granted to masons, but they all appear to have been retaining fees paid to master masons, or bridge masons, and not infirmity or old age

[1] *Exch. R.*, ii, 477.   [2] *Aberdeen*, i, 41–2, 52, 68.
[3] The accounts show several cases of masons hired for a year.
[4] *Rentale Dunkeldense*, 123.   [5] Contract printed in Mylne, 63–4.
[6] *Ayr*, 268.   [7] H. and W., 40–1.
[8] M.o.W. A/cs., xxix, fo. 90.
[9] *Ayr*, 265. This may have been pure charity, and not a payment because the mason had been formerly employed by the burgh.
[10] H. and W., 40–1.   [11] *Treas. A/cs.*, x, 160.

pensions, such as can occasionally be traced among English masons.

That working masons were not always satisfied with the conditions under which they worked is shown by the fact that on occasion they withheld, or threatened to withhold, their labour, until an improvement had been effected. Thus, in the spring of 1634, labour difficulties appear to have delayed work at the Parliament House, Edinburgh,[1] and in the autumn of 1638, certain layers at the Tron Kirk, Edinburgh, refused to work, unless their wages were raised from £3 12s. 0d. to £4 a week.[2] Two years earlier, an employer at Lochwinnoch complained that "when all the wallers had wrought 6 days, they gave over the work and would not lay one stone more, except a new price which I was forced to give them, 8 marks. And it pleased them not. But every day of fifteen I gave them two quarts of ale, which was £4."[3]

Wages.—The available information is unfortunately but slight, especially prior to 1530. For the first half of the fourteenth century, our only figures relate to Edinburgh Castle in 1335–7 and to Stirling Castle in 1336–7. At the former, fifteen masons were in receipt of 6d. a day, five of 5d., and six of 4d.[4]; at the latter, five masons were paid 3s. 6d. a week.[5] On the assumption that the masons at Stirling worked seven days a week, which is not improbable in view of the urgency of placing the castle in a better state of defence, the predominant rate at Edinburgh and Stirling appears to have been 6d. a day, which compares very favourably with contemporary English figures.[6]

---

[1] H. and W., 30.

[2] Building Account under date 16 September, 1638.

[3] R. W. Postgate, *The Builders' History*, 3. We have modernised the orthography.

[4] *Cal. Doc. Scot.*, iii, 347.   [5] *Ibid.*, iii, 364.

[6] The predominant wage in England in the first half of the fourteenth century was 4d. a day; at the repair of Beaumaris Castle in 1330 it was 4⅔d. (*The Mediaeval Mason*, 236). At this period no allowance has to be made for the depreciation of the pound Scots in terms of sterling (Henderson, 16), but it is probable that the wages quoted, being paid at Edinburgh and Stirling, were in terms of sterling, as they occur in an Enlgish document; in either case, assuming price levels were fairly equal in the two countries,

For the fifteenth century, the few wage rates that we have been able to trace, either in building accounts, or in contracts, were generally expressed as so much per annum, and in some cases, such as those at Cupar-Angus Abbey referred to previously, were undoubtedly in addition to food.[1] At Aberdeen, the rates paid were 20 marks a year in 1484 and 1493, and 18, 21 and 22 marks a year in 1498.[2] At the erection of Dunkeld Bridge from 1510 to 1516, the predominant annual wages paid to masons were £10, £12 and £13 6s. 8d., though in one case the annual stipend was as low as 10 marks, and in two others as high as £13 6s. 8d. *plus* 8 bolls of meal, and £15 6s. 8d. How the weekly wage, corresponding to one of these annual stipends, should be calculated is uncertain, as we do not know what allowance to make for holidays, or for winter cessation of work. The only definite information we have relates to a certain John Wyis, a mason employed for two weeks at Dunkeld Bridge at 6s. a week in June, 1510, and then engaged for a year at 10 marks per annum. In this case, a year was treated as equivalent to approximately 22 weeks of full-time employment.[3] If this same factor of 22 weeks is applied to other annual stipends at Dunkeld, and to those at Aberdeen, then a sum of £10 per annum was equivalent to 9s. a week; £12, or 18 marks, to 10s. 9d.; £13 6s. 8d., or 20 marks, to 12s.; and 22 marks to 13s. 3d. As these figures harmonise quite well with such weekly

masons were being paid distinctly more in Scotland than in England. Very possibly our samples of Scottish rates were not typical, being cases of payments in Scotland by the English Crown, at a time when there was war between the two countries.

[1] *Cupar*, i, 304, 307, 309. A mason employed at Dingwall Castle in 1504–7, received for the year £3, 1 chalder of flour and 8 bolls of barley (*Exch. R.*, xii, 238, 514, 551).

[2] *Aberdeen*, i, 41–2, 52, 68.

[3] At Eton College, about 1445, church holidays reduced the working year to 45 weeks of full-time employment; at Rochester Castle in 1368, holidays and cessation of work in winter reduced the setters' working year to 30 weeks of full-time employment. A possible indication that little building was done during the winter in Scotland is the instruction, in November 1648, with regard to the steeple of St. Giles, Edinburgh. The dean of gild was ordered to get materials ready during the winter so that the masons might start work in the spring. (*Edinburgh*, 1642–5, 180).

THE SCOTTISH MASON

TABLE OF MONEY WAGES (WITHOUT FOOD, IN SUMMER)

Year.	Place.	Weekly Wages.		Corresponding Weekly Wages in England.[2]
		In Scottish Money.	Approx. Equivalent in Sterling.[1]	
1501	Edinburgh [3]	9s., 10s.	2s. 3d., 2s. 6d.	3s.
1510	Dunkeld [4]	6s.	1s. 6d.	3s.
1515	Dunkeld [5]	10s.	2s. 6d.	3s.
1529–30	Edinburgh [6]	10s., 14s., 15s.	2s.6d., 3s.6d.,3s.9d.	3s.
1534–35	Linlithgow [7]	12s., 14s., 16s.	3s., 3s. 6d., 4s.	3s. 6d.
1535–36	Edinburgh [8]	12s., 13s., 14s., 15s.	3s., 3s. 3d., 3s. 6d., 3s. 9d.	3s. 6d.
1537–38	Falkland [9]	10s., 12s., 14s.	2s. 6d., 3s., 3s. 6d.	3s. 6d.
1541–42	Ayr [10]	12s. to 20s.	3s. to 5s.	3s. 6d.
1545–46	Edinburgh [11]	16s.	4s.	3s. 6d.
1552–53	Edinburgh [12]	18s.	4s. 6d.	5s.
1553–54	Edinburgh [13]	18s., 20s.	4s. 6d., 5s.	5s.
1554–55	Edinburgh [14]	17s., 18s., 20s.	4s. 3d., 4s. 6d., 5s.	5s.
1555–56	Edinburgh [15]	18s., 20s.	4s. 6d., 5s.	5s.
1591–92	Ayr [16]	36s. 8d. to 52s.	4s. 7d. to 6s. 6d.	6s.
1594–95	Ayr [17]	60s.	6s.	6s.
1596	Edinburgh [18]	50s.	5s.	6s.
1598–99	Ayr [19]	56s. 8d.	5s. 8d.	6s.
1599	Edinburgh [20]	67s.	6s. 7d.	6s.
1600–01	Ayr [21]	56s. 8d., 60s.	5s. 8d., 6s.	6s.
1613	Edinburgh [22]	60s.	5s.	6s.
1615	Edinburgh [23]	72s.	6s.	6s.
1616	Edinburgh [24]	72s., 80s.	6s., 6s. 8d.	6s.
1617	Edinburgh [25]	72s.	6s.	6s.
1617–18	Edinburgh [26]	72s., 86s. 8d.	6s., 7s. 3d.	6s.
1626	Edinburgh [27]	72s.	6s.	7s.
1628	Linlithgow [28]	72s.	6s.	7s.
1637–38	Edinburgh [29]	72s. 80s.	6s., 6s. 8d.	7s.
1639	Edinburgh [30]	84s.	6s. 8d.	7s.
1666	Panmure House [31]	100s., 106s. 8d.	8s. 4d., 8s. 10d.	9s.

[1] Converted on the basis of figures given in Henderson, which relate to particular years. Consequently, for the sixteenth century our equivalents are only approximate. [2] Calculated from the table given in our *Mediaeval Mason*, 236. [3] *Edinburgh, 1403–1528*, 90. [4] Mylne, 24. [5] *Ibid.*, 29. [6] M.o.W. A/cs., i. [7] *Ibid.*, iv. [8] *Ibid.*, iv. [9] *Ibid.*, v. [10] Ayr, 89. [11] *Treas. A/cs.*, viii, 441–2, 447. [12] *Edinburgh, 1528–57*, 278. [13] *Ibid.*, 288, 346. [14] *Ibid.*, 298, 302, 303. [15] *Ibid.*, 319, 322. [16] Ayr, 174. [17] *Ibid.*, 186. [18] *Edinburgh, 1589–1603*, 354. [19] Ayr, 198. [20] *Edinburgh, 1589–1603*, 370. [21] Ayr, 205. [22] M.o.W. A/cs., x. [23] *Ibid.*, xi. [24] *Ibid.*, xy. [25] Mylne, 106. [26] *Ibid.*, 107. [27] *Ibid.*, 73. [28] *Ibid.*, 118. [29] Tron Kirk A/cs. [30] M.o.W. A/cs., xxix. [31] Mylne, 154.

wage rates as we have been able to ascertain for the first part of the sixteenth century, we are disposed to think that the factor 22, for converting annual stipends into weekly wage rates, is fairly reliable for this period. Nevertheless, we have not incorporated in our table any weekly wage-rates originally quoted as annual stipends, for fear that the estimated weekly equivalents might be misleading.

Such weekly wage rates as we have been able to ascertain for the sixteenth and seventeenth centuries have been incorporated in the table opposite, in which we give the year and place of payment of each particular wage, and the equivalent in sterling. In the few cases where our sources indicate daily rates, we have converted them into weekly rates by multiplying by six, in order to secure uniformity. For purposes of comparison, we have added a column showing the corresponding weekly wages in England, excluding London. It must be borne in mind that all the figures relate to money wages; to interpret the nominal Scottish figures, allowance must be made (i) for the increasing depreciation of the pound Scots in terms of sterling and (ii) for changes in the cost of living. In the absence of material from which an index number of Scottish food prices can be calculated,[1] it is necessary to adopt the somewhat rough and ready expedient of assuming that, apart from the effect of currency debasement, food prices rose to a similar extent in Scotland and in England, a not improbable assumption in so far as such rise was brought about by the great influx of precious metals from America into Europe.

The table shows that money wages in Scotland rose from 10s. to 100s. a week between 1501 and 1666. This great nominal rise is partly explained by the growing depreciation of the pound Scots, which had fallen from about one-fourth of its nominal value in sterling in 1501 to one-twelfth in 1666. Thus the rise from 10s. to 100s. Scots was equivalent to a rise from 2s. 6d. to 8s. 4d. sterling. During the same period, weekly wages in England rose from 3s. to 9s. This increase in England was accounted for, and more than accounted for, by the great rise in price

---

[1] Cf. Henderson, 10.

levels, food costing roughly five times as much in 1666 as it did in 1500. When this is allowed for, we find that the mason's wage in 1666, viz., 9*s*., would purchase only about three-fifths of what the mason's wage in 1500, viz., 3*s*., would purchase. There can be little doubt that the same sort of thing was true of Scotland; 100*s*. Scots (or 8*s*. 4*d*. sterling) would purchase considerably less in 1666 than would 10*s*. Scots (or 2*s*. 6*d*. sterling) in 1500, though exactly how much less we are unable to say for want of the necessary evidence. If the English figures are accepted as a guide, then the Scottish mason's wage in 1666, viz., 100*s*. Scots, would purchase only about two-thirds of what the Scottish mason's wage in 1501, viz., 10*s*. Scots, would purchase.[1]

At the head of the table we have described the wage rates as "without food, in summer". We do not exclude "drink", because we cannot be sure that "drink" was not provided in some cases at least, either on special occasions, or even systematically. Payments of "drinksilver" to masons and other craftsmen occur frequently in the *Lord High Treasurer's Accounts*,[2] generally with no indication as to the reason. In 1515, however, in connection with works at Inchegarvey, the payment of 56*s*. at diverse times in drinksilver to the masons is stated to have been at the "up-putting of the lintels and for the expedition of their labours and diligence".[3] Similarly, at the repair of the College at St. Andrews in 1683–90, ale was provided for the masons at the putting on of every lintel, at the placing of every keystone, and at the capping of each chimney.[4] More systematic allowance for drink appears to have been made at Ayr in 1591–2, and at Edinburgh in 1610. At Ayr, where the masons were paid 36*s*. 8*d*. to 52*s*. a week, each, in addition, was allowed 8*s*. 8*d*. or 10*s*. a week "for morning and afternoon drink and Sunday meat".[5] At Edinburgh

---

[1] If, after making allowance for the depreciation of the pound Scots in terms of sterling, and for price changes in both countries (which actually may have been different), Scottish wage rates are compared with English wage rates, the possibility that English masons were able to earn their wages for more weeks in the year than Scottish masons must not be overlooked.

[2] E.g., i, 116, 300, 354, 369; ii, 97, 103, 104, 109, 118, 124, 128, 137.

[3] *Ibid.*, v, 24.   [4] Fleming, 244.   [5] *Ayr*, 174.

in 1610, the Town Council fixed the wage of a master mason at £4 a week and of a qualified servant at 4 marks (53s. 4d.) a week, and 6s. 8d. for drink and drinksilver.[1] Towards the end of the seventeenth century, the practice of supplying food and drink to workmen at the morning and afternoon breaks was described by one writer [2] as "the custom long ago", so that at one time it was probably much more prevalent than the few examples we have quoted would suggest. The fact previously mentioned, that many building contracts stipulated for payments to mason-contractors partly in kind, presumably implies that the workmen in their turn were paid partly in kind by the mason-contractors. In so far as this was the case, they would escape some, at least, of the burden of rising prices.

Apart from the provision of food or drink, a mason's money wage might be supplemented by the free provision of accommodation. Thus at the building of the quay at Ayr, the house rent of the masons was paid in 1599–1600 and 1601–2.[3] At the erection of Panmure House in 1666, it was stipulated in the contract that the Earl was to provide the masons with houses for their lodging.

Regarding summer and winter rates we have very little information, and cannot be sure what happened when masons were employed in the middle of winter. At Falkland Palace, in the autumn of 1538,[4] John Brownhill, master mason, and his three servants were paid 50s. a week, and James Blake, mason, and his three servants, 46s. a week. For the five weeks commencing November 2nd, Brownhill and his three servants were paid 44s. a week (instead of 50s.), but Blake and his three servants still

---

[1] *Edinburgh, 1604–26*, 61. This assessment was apparently made under an Act of 1426 (*Laws*, 10) which authorised town councils to fix the fees of masons, wrights and other workmen who handled materials belonging to other men. Another example of municipal assessment of wages in the building industry occurred at Aberdeen in 1648, when, "considering the exorbitant prices taken by the slaters", the Council ordained that each master should have 24s. a day without meat and drink, every man that worked with the trowel, 12s. daily; and a carrier of lime 6s. 8d. daily, all without meat and drink "except these they work to sall be pleasit of thair oune accord" (*Aberdeen, 1643–1747*, 89).

[2] Strathmore, 80.   [3] *Ayr*, 201, 205, 210.   [4] M.o.W. A/cs., v.

received 46s. a week, so that if there was a reduction for short hours in winter, it does not appear to have applied universally. At Edinburgh Castle from November, 1616, to February, 1617, two masons normally in receipt of £4 and £3 a week, were paid only £3 and 45s., or three-quarters of their usual rates.[1] At the re-erection of the City Cross at Edinburgh, six master masons were paid £4 a week each, and eight other masons 50s. a week each, in January, 1617–18, whereas the following month the master masons received £4 13s. 4d. a week each, and the other masons 72s.[2] Assuming that the January figures were winter rates and the February figures summer rates (winter rates from November 1st to February 2nd being fairly common in England), then, in winter, the summer rates were reduced by some 15 per cent in the case of master masons and by some 30 per cent in the case of other masons. In the Panmure House building contract of 1666, it was provided that during the winter, when the masons were to be employed in hewing stones, the wages were to be reduced by one-quarter.[3]

Hours of Labour.—No information is available for the period before the sixteenth century, when the hours appear to have been very similar to those worked in England. At Stirling in 1529, the summer hours were 5 a.m. to 7 p.m., with half an hour for "disjone" at 8.30, two hours for dinner at 11, and half an hour for "nunshankis" at 3.30. During the remainder of the year, "when the day is short", the hours were from daylight to 11.30, and from 1.00 to evening.[4] At Dundee in 1537, the summer hours were from 5 a.m. to 7 p.m., with half an hour for "disjune" at 8.30, one and a half hours for dinner at 11.30, and half an hour for "none-shanks" at 4 o'clock. "When the days be short" the masons were to commence work as soon as they could see, with a single break of one and a half hours at midday from November 1st to February 2nd, and with

---

[1] M.o.W. A/cs., xv.   [2] Accounts printed in Mylne, 106, 107.

[3] In England, wages were commonly reduced one-sixth in winter (*The Mediaeval Mason*, 118). The winter's day would be somewhat longer in England than in Scotland.

[4] *Stirling*, 35–7.

the usual three breaks during the rest of the year.[1] At Edinburgh in 1610, the summer hours were 5–8, 9–12, 1–4, 4.30–7;[2] at Panmure House in 1666, they were 5–8, 9–12, 1.30–4, 4.30–7.[3]

Towards the end of the seventeenth century, or early in the eighteenth, some modification of these hours appears to have been made. At Glasgow, in 1746, it was stated that journeyman servants of the craft, "past memory of man", had been used to work from 6 a.m. to 7 p.m., allowing a reasonable time for breakfast and dinner, but that of late many journeyman had agreed among themselves to work only from 6 to 6, claiming full wages as formerly. As a consequence, it was decided by the Masons' Incorporation that in future no freeman of the trade should hire any journeyman except on the accustomed terms, i.e., 6 a.m. to 7 p.m., with one hour each for breakfast and dinner.[4]

As early as 1474 we have noted a monastic carpenter at Arbroath, whose hours were 7 to 7, both in summer and winter,[5] but whether these hours applied to masons and other monastic craftsmen at Arbroath, or whether they applied to carpenters outside the abbey, there is no evidence to show.

Holidays.—For want of continuous weekly or fortnightly building accounts, showing individual wages, we are unable to trace the extent to which the numerous saints' days and church festivals were observed in Scotland prior to the Reformation, nor, apart from the case of annual engagements, do we know whether it was the practice to pay wages in respect of such holidays. If we may judge by a statute of 1493, masons claimed their wages for holidays as well as workdays, although it was illegal to do so.[6] At Stirling in 1529, it was provided that no holiday was to be observed or claimed but those commanded by law [7]; according to a statute of 1469, masons and wrights were to keep no more holidays than those laid down by the Church as

---

[1] Extracted from contract of service of Geo. Boiss, printed in Mylne, 63–4.
[2] *Edinburgh, 1604–26*, 61. [3] Extracted from Panmure House contract.
[4] *Glasgow, 1739–59*, 226–8. [5] *Register of the Abbey of Arbroath*, 171.
[6] *Laws*, 51. [7] *Stirling*, 35–6.

great solemn feasts.[1]   At Dundee in 1537, it was stipulated that masons were to work on the eves of festivals till 4 o'clock, except at Christmas, Easter, Whitsun and the Assumption of our Lady (Aug. 15), when work was to cease at 12 o'clock.[2]   This appears to have been slightly more liberal than the act of 1469, which provided that masons, whether engaged for long periods or short, should work on Saturdays and other eves of festivals till 4 p.m., under penalty of deductions from their wages.[3]

Tools.—References to tools are neither detailed nor numerous, but they relate to a fairly long period, and to different parts of Scotland. At Edinburgh Castle in 1337,[4] at Kildrummy in 1438,[5] at Dunkeld Bridge in 1513,[6] at Inchegarvey in 1515,[7] at Holyroodhouse in 1529–30,[8] at Ayr in 1597 and 1599–1600,[9] and at Glasgow in 1626,[10] the employers appear to have been responsible for providing or sharpening the masons' "irons". Whether masons' axes or hammers were generally provided or mended by the employers, there is not sufficient evidence to show.

Gloves.—The practice of supplying masons with gloves, which can be traced in England as early as the fourteenth century, appears to have been observed to some extent at least in Scotland in the seventeenth century, as, for example, at Ayr in 1598–9 and 1599–1600,[11] at Edinburgh in 1637,[12] and at St. Andrews in 1684, 1687 and 1688.[13]   The object of the gloves being to protect the layers' hands from splinters, it is noteworthy that in the summer of 1637 at the erection of the Parliament House, Edinburgh, gloves were distributed to the whole company "of the hewaris of the

---

[1] *Laws*, 33.   [2] Mylne, 64.   [3] *Laws*, 33.

[4] *Cal. Doc. Scot.*, iii, 357, records the purchase of iron for masons' tools.

[5] Iron purchased and the smith paid for making masons' tools and irons (*Exch. R.*, v, 58).

[6] Smith paid for sharpening quarry irons and repairing apprentices' irons.

[7] Smith paid for making and mending masons' irons (*Treas. A/cs.*, v, 24).

[8] Payment for sharpening picks (M.o.W. A/cs., i).

[9] Smiths paid for sharpening masons' irons (*Ayr*, 194, 203).

[10] A smith undertook to sharpen the masons' irons during the building of the Tolbooth, for a sum of £40 paid by the Town Council (Cruikshank, 70).

[11] *Ayr*, 198, 201, 203.   [12] H. and W., 54.   [13] Fleming, 244.

maissounis" ;[1] this seems to bear out our previous conten-
tion that there was little or no dividing line between hewers
and layers in Scotland. In the autumn of 1637, however,
gloves were given at the same building operation to the
masons "that laid upon the wall",[2] which suggests that
there were some masons engaged solely in laying.

Apprenticeship.—The earliest references to the apprenticeship of masons in Scotland which we have been able to
trace relate to the binding of apprentices at the Cistercian
Abbey of Cupar-Angus, Forfarshire, in 1466 and subsequent years. Between 1466 and 1497, the *Rental Book* of
the Abbey shows that eleven youths were apprenticed to the
mason craft, others being bound to carpenters, smiths and
tilers.[3] Of the eleven youths, five were engaged as apprentices to the monastery, it being indicated in three of these
cases under whom they were to work; six are stated to have
become apprentices to particular masons, all of whom were
probably in the regular employment of the monastery,
although we know this for certain only of two of the
men. At Durham Priory in 1488, we find a mason named
John Bell, who was entitled to have an apprentice of his
own and was, at the same time, according to his contract,
to teach and inform an apprentice of the Priory in the
mason craft.[4] It may well be that at Cupar-Angus both
types of apprentice were also to be found, that is (i) monastic
apprentices and (ii) apprentices bound to monastic craftsmen. The terms on which the apprentices were engaged
varied: of the eleven apprentice masons, one was bound for
5 years, one for 6, five for 7, three for 9, and in one instance
the period is not specified. In the case of two apprentice
carpenters bound for 7 years, it is recorded that they were
to receive the common and usual service in victual and other
things, and as wages one mark yearly for the first three
years, 20s. for the next two, and 2 marks for the last two.
An apprentice tiler, bound for 8 years, in addition to the
common service or food of the monastery, was to have as

---

[1] H. and W., 54.   [2] *Ibid.*, 54.   [3] *Cupar*, i, 304–10.
[4] *Hist. Dunelm Scriptores Tres* (Surtees Soc.), ccclxxxiii; prior to 1488,
the date of Bell's contract, monastic apprentices can be traced at Durham
in 1483–4 and 1485–6 (*Durham Account Rolls* [Surtees Soc.], ii, 415, 416).

wage 2 marks yearly for the first four years, and 30s. yearly for the remaining four years. The apprentice mason bound for 5 years was to have victuals "according to the custom of apprentices", and for wages 20s. per annum for the first three years, and 2 marks for the last two years. In the case of the other apprentice masons, the terms of remuneration are either not stated in the printed version of the Rental Book, or are described "as in other similar engagements".[1]

A somewhat similar case to that of a monastic craftsman taking an apprentice occurred at Dundee. By the terms of the appointment of George Boiss as mason for life to the Kirk of Our Lady and to the town works of Dundee in 1537,[2] it was provided that he should have an apprentice from 7 years to 7 years, another to be taken as the time of one expired. Boiss was to receive nothing in respect of an apprentice during his first year, and £10 per annum (equivalent to five-twelfths of his own wage) during the remaining six years.

The other main sources of information about apprentices are municipal and similar regulations. The seal of cause of the masons and wrights of Edinburgh, granted 15 October, 1475,[3] provided, *inter alia*, that no master or person of the two crafts was to take an apprentice for less than seven years; that when an apprentice had finished his term, he was to be examined by the four searchers of the masons and wrights and, if found proficient, was to be admitted a fellow of the craft. If not found proficient, he was to serve a master until he was worthy, and was then to be made a freeman and fellow. At Glasgow, the seal of cause of the masons and wrights, granted in 1551,[4] provided that no craftsman should have more than one apprentice at a time, or for a shorter period than seven years. It would appear, however, from minutes of the Incorporation of Masons, of 9 February, 1613, and 5 February, 1617, that nine years was the customary period of apprenticeship,

---

[1] The money portions of the wage payments were doubtless paid to the masters or instructors of the apprentices, as is clearly indicated in the contract of George Boiss at Dundee, mentioned in the next paragraph.

[2] Contract printed in Mylne, 63–4.

[3] *Edinburgh, 1403–1538*, 31–2.   [4] Cruikshank, 3 *folg*.

namely, "seven years to learn the trade and two for meat and fee".[1] In an earlier minute of 11 December, 1600, it was laid down that no freeman should have more than one servant at a time and one apprentice who has served his term.[2] The Schaw Statutes of 1598, which applied generally to masons in Scotland, provided, *inter alia*, that no master should take more than three apprentices during his lifetime without special permission; that an apprentice should be bound for at least seven years, and that, except by special permission, a further period of seven years should elapse before he could be made a fellow of the craft.   At Lanark, where a new seal of cause was granted to the masons and wrights in 1674,[3] it was provided that no craftsman was to take an apprentice for a shorter period than three years, and that no apprentice was to be admitted as a freeman without serving as a journeyman to a freeman for two years after the expiration of his apprenticeship. The Laws and Statutes of the Lodge of Aberdeen, 1670,[4] show that three years had to elapse between the termination of an apprenticeship and reception into the fellowship. During this interval between ceasing to be an apprentice and becoming a fellow, which appears to have been a widespread arrangement in Scotland in the seventeenth century, the ex-apprentice was called an entered apprentice.[5] When the category of entered apprentices, intermediate between apprentices and fellows, was first established, is uncertain ; it did not exist in Edinburgh in 1475, if we may judge by the seal of cause of that year; on the other hand, the Schaw Statutes of 1598 imply it, and other evidence also suggests that it existed prior to 1598.[6] The system

---

[1] Cruikshank, 63.   [2] *Ibid.*, 63.   [3] *Lanark*, 196.

[4] Printed in Miller, 57 *folg*. The seals of cause granted to the masons at Aberdeen in 1527 and 1541 contain no provisions relating to apprenticeship, apart from the fees to be paid in respect of new apprentices (Bain, 238–40).

[5] Cf. "The Mason Word", p. 87 below.

[6] Cf. *ibid.*, p. 92 below; also R. J. Meekren, "The Aitchison's Haven Minutes and Early Scottish Free Masonry" (shortly to appear in *A.Q.C.*), a paper which we first saw after the Prestonian Lecture had been dispatched to the printer. By a detailed analysis of the printed version of the Minutes (*A.Q.C.*, xxiv), he reaches, quite independently, conclusions very similar to

doubtless represented an attempt to check the number of potential masters, as did the regulations limiting the number of apprentices a master might have. The same is probably true of an Edinburgh regulation of 1576, which provided that no craftsman was to be admitted a burgess without his indenture of apprenticeship and certificate of good service, entry in the craft book not being sufficient evidence.[1] It is not unlikely that all these devices were introduced in the sixteenth century, a period when gilds tended to develop restrictive policies.

Relatively early instances of mason apprentices occur at Linlithgow Palace, Dunkeld Bridge and Holyroodhouse. At Linlithgow, a mason named Stephen Balty (Stewin Bawtee) appears to have been on regular maintenance work at the Palace from 1512 to 1516. An apprentice worked with him all the time, and for part of the time either one, or two, masons assisted him.[2] Two apprentices, James Aysone and John Dyikes, were employed at Dunkeld Bridge in 1511–13, the cost of their clothing, fee (? pocket money) and of their instruction, being charged to the Bridge account, and the cost of their food to the Abbey account,[3] so that they were almost certainly Abbey apprentices. At Holyroodhouse in August, 1529, fourteen masons were employed, including at the end of the list in the Account, "Wa. Graham prentys". The payment entered against his name was 6s. a week, the standard rate being apparently 15s.[4] There is nothing to show whose apprentice he was, but it is not unlikely that he was bound to John Aitone, the master mason.

A relatively late reference to apprentices shows that the

ours concerning the position of entered apprentices in Scottish operative masonry, and the probability that entered apprentices and fellowcrafts had distinct sets of secrets in 1598.

[1] *Edinburgh, 1573–89*, 49.

[2] In 1512–13 he was paid 14s. a week for 52 weeks in respect of himself and his apprentice (*Treas. A/cs.*, iv, 279) and in the autumn of 1513 he was in receipt of the same rate of remuneration (*ibid.*, iv, 525). In 1514 he was paid £29 13s. 4d. for his fee and that of his apprentice, and in 1515 £30 (*Exch. R.*, xiv, 48, 94). In 1516, a sum of £15 was entered as paid to the late Stephen Balty (*ibid.*, xiv, 94).

[3] *Rentale Dunkeldense*, 123.   [4] M.o.W. A/cs., i.

system of wage payments had undergone considerable modification, bringing it much more into line with the English system, by which the wage payment, instead of being uniform throughout the term, tended to rise with the seniority of the apprentice. In the Panmure House building contract of 1666, it was provided that the weekly wages of the apprentices should be 24s., if of one year's standing; 40s., if of two years' standing; £3 12s. 0d., if of three years' standing; and £5, if of more than three years' standing. £5, without meat and drink, was the weekly wage of ordinary masons at Panmure House, a few of the senior men receiving £5 6s. 8d.

Recruitment.—How masons for any particular building operation were recruited, if enough local men were not available, is uncertain, but where masons entered into contracts to erect work away from home, it is not unlikely that the mason-contractors took some of their men with them. Thus we find a Dundee mason contracting to do work at Newtyle, Forfarshire, in 1589;[1] a Kilwinning mason at Partick, Glasgow, in 1611;[2] a Dundee mason at Falkland in 1620;[3] a Nairne mason at Cawdor in 1639;[4] and an Edinburgh mason at Dreel, Fifeshire, in 1663.[5]

In some cases, the master craftsmen, working with their men away from home, do not appear to have been contractors on task work, but workmen on day or weekly wages. Thus in March, 1503, John Brown, mason, was paid a quarter's fee of £10 for himself and his man, when he came from Falkland to work at Holyroodhouse.[6] Among other "master masons" and masons in receipt of weekly wages at Holyroodhouse in 1535–6, we find "Andrew Vilertoun, master mason of Perth, and the remaining four masons with him";[7] among the "master masons" and masons employed at Falkland Palace in 1537–38, "Moyse Martyn, master mason of Dunbar, and his servant"[8] were paid for five weeks at 30s. a week. At Dunkeld in 1507–8, wages were paid to four stone masons of Perth and their servants, and to two stone masons of Perth and their servants.[9]

[1] Mylne, 66–8.   [2] M. and R., v, 5.   [3] Mylne, 110, 111.
[4] *Cawdor*, 283.   [5] M. and R., v, 554.   [6] *Treas. A/cs.*, ii, 271.
[7] M.o.W. A/cs., iv.   [8] *Ibid.*, v.   [9] *Rentale Dunkeldense*, 170.

There is evidence in the surviving building accounts, relating both to large and small operations, which points to individual masons being recruited from a distance during the course of particular jobs. (i) In numerous cases messengers, or masons, or overseers, were paid their expenses "seeking masons", either without reference to the locality, as in the Edinburgh Castle accounts in 1615–16 [1] and the Falkland Palace accounts in 1628–9,[2] or, as was more usual, with an indication where the men were to be sought. Thus masons were sought in Perth for Dunkeld Bridge in 1515 and for Holyroodhouse in 1535–6;[3] in Edinburgh for Falkland Palace in 1504;[4] in Dingwall for work at Darnaway in 1501;[5] in Stirling, Paisley, Glasgow and Renfrewshire for work at Dumbarton about 1619;[6] in Dunbar for work at Haddington in 1547–8.[7] (ii) In some building accounts there are entries which show that the expenses of masons coming from outside were defrayed, as for instance, the expenses of masons coming from Elgin to Inverness in 1460;[8] the cost of transporting the tackle of four masons from Melrose to Edinburgh in 1615–16;[9] and similar costs of Edinburgh masons to Stirling in 1625.[10] (iii) In other cases, the costs paid were those of masons returning home in the autumn at the end of the building season. Thus at Edinburgh Castle in 1616, "at the upgiving of the works", payments were made to masons returning to Stirling, Linlithgow, Dunfermline, Glasgow, and "to the parts where they dwelt";[11] at Stirling in 1625, there was paid the cost of transport home in the autumn of masons to Edinburgh and of slaters to Dundee.[12]

On some occasions at least, while England and Scotland were separate, English masons were employed in Scotland. During Edward III's campaigns in Scotland, following the death of Robert Bruce in 1329, English masons were impressed in Norfolk and Suffolk for work at Dunnottar Castle in 1336;[13] and a surviving account of

[1] M.o.W. A/cs., xi.   [2] M. and R., v, 551.   [3] M.o.W. A/cs., iv.
[4] *Treas. A/cs.*, ii, 418.   [5] *Ibid.*, ii, 126.
[6] M. and R., v, 549, 550.   [7] *Treas. A/cs.*, ix, 154.
[8] *Exch. R.*, vi, 656.   [9] M.o.W. A/cs., x.   [10] Mylne, 72.
[11] M.o.W. A/cs., x.   [12] Mylne, 73.   [13] M. and R., v, 524.

Edinburgh Castle shows that nineteen English masons, together with ten Scottish masons and quarriers, were employed there in 1337.[1] At later dates, we find evidence of foreign masons in Scotland. Thus in 1511 and 1512, an Italian mason was in receipt of £7 a month for wages, expenses and fees.[2] In 1539, the expenses were paid of four French masons on one occasion, and of six French masons on another, sent to the King by the Duke of Guise.[3] Further, the Falkland Palace accounts show that a French master mason was employed there for many months in 1540 and 1541, at a monthly wage of £3 6s. 8d.[4] It was not only on royal jobs, however, that foreign masons were employed. Flemish masons were engaged by the municipality of Edinburgh to repair St. Giles Church in the summer of 1599. The burgh accounts show that the town paid a sum of 42s. "spent in Middleburgh drinking with them [i.e., the Flemish masons] before they agreed to come"; that daily wages of 30s. were paid to Lawrence the Fleming, mason, and 15s. to Hans, his workman, in addition to drinksilver amounting to 6s. 8d. a day for the pair; and that in due course their passages home were paid.[5]

The foregoing reference to the impressment of masons in Norfolk and Suffolk in 1336 raises the question to what extent, if any, a system of impressment prevailed in Scotland. Mention has already been made of the practice of "seeking masons" at a distance; what compulsion, if any, was behind such "seeking" there is little or no evidence to show. We have, however, traced one or two indications of some measure of compulsion: thus on 14 April, 1501, a payment was made "to Richard Wallas to pass *with the King's writing* to Melrose for two masons to the Kirk of Steil".[6] The expression *with the King's writing* certainly suggests some kind of order. In 1513, very possibly in connection with the campaign at Flodden, we find a series

---

[1] *Cal. Doc. Scot.*, iii, 361.   [2] *Treas. A/cs.*, iv, 271, 439.
[3] *Ibid.*, vii, 48, 184.
[4] *Ibid.*, vii, 330, 394, 405, 415, 422, 431, 439, 446, 450, 456, 462, 472.
[5] *Edinburgh, 1589–1603*, 369, 370.
[6] *Treas. A/cs.*, ii, 103.   The italics are ours.

of similar entries in the *Accounts of the Lord High Treasurer*, of which the first may be quoted as an example:

> George Aleis, mason, and 12 servants with him to pass in[to] England *at the King's command* . £27.[1]

Service in England *at the King's command* would seem to imply compulsion. The terms of the life contract of service of George Boiss, mason, at Dundee in 1537 appear to contemplate the possibility of his being called upon to work for the King or other lord.[2] So also does the contract of John Kowtis, appointed master mason at Stirling in 1529.[3]

Although these instances do seem to us to point to a practice of impressment in Scotland, the system apparently operated on a very much smaller scale than in England, unless it be that evidence of it is lost. We have traced no further instance of the practice until 1599, when the burgh of Dumfries was ordered to send twenty-four pioneers and masons for a military expedition.[4] In July, 1604, an act was passed compelling masons to come and build the ruinous parts of Holyroodhouse.[5] In 1617, an order was issued by the Privy Council, very possibly under the act of 1604, for certain masons from Dundee, St. Andrews, Dysart, Pittenweem, Culross, Preston, Glasgow and Linlithgow to come with their tools to Holyroodhouse to assist in the repairs, under pain of being regarded as rebels.[6] As in England in an earlier period, complete success did not attend the effort, and the records show that several of the masons summoned from St. Andrews failed to present themselves at Holyroodhouse.[7]

Free and Unfree Craftsmen.—Although it seems probable

---

[1] *Treas, A/cs.*, iv., 520–1. The italics are ours.

[2] The following is an extract from the contract (Mylne, 64): "Also gif it happen the said George *be chargit*, or the town requirit for him, *to the King's werk*, or to ony other lord's or gentleman's werks, in that case the said George ... sall have na fee of the town nor their maister of werks." The italics are ours.

[3] *Stirling*, 36. The municipality's licence was necessary for Kowtis to work for other employers, "saiffand the Kingis grace allegiance alanerlye owttane [alone excepted]".

[4] *Reg. P.C.*, vi, 27.

[5] *Ibid.*, vii, 9.

[6] *Ibid.*, xi, 25–6.

[7] *Ibid.*, xi, 63.

that impressment played but a small part in the life of the Scottish mason in the sixteenth and seventeenth centuries, there is plenty of evidence to show that masons at that period not infrequently worked in burghs other than those in which they normally dwelt, either because their employer obtained a contract there, or as a result of being sought, or very possibly of their own accord. This raises the question of the position of craftsmen working in burghs in which, presumably, they did not enjoy the freedom. The information available for the discussion of this question is unfortunately somewhat limited. By an Act of Parliament passed in 1540,[1] anyone with buildings to erect was authorised to employ good craftsmen, freemen or others, because of the extortionate charges of craftsmen, especially in the burghs. There is little or no evidence to show how far the act, which was confirmed in 1607,[2] was effective. We cannot find any direct reference to the subject of free and unfree masons outside Edinburgh, Glasgow and Aberdeen,[3] the principal burghs, so far as we know, which possessed incorporations of masons and wrights,[4] and possibly, therefore, the principal burghs in which masons enjoyed an officially recognised monopoly of trade.

In the case of the oldest incorporation, that of Edinburgh, established by seal of cause in 1475, there was no provision in the original regulations in favour of freemen.[5] The only requirement was that if a craftsman came to the burgh and desired work, he must first satisfy the overseers of the Incorporation that he was competent, and, if approved, pay a mark towards the maintenance of the altar. In the sixteenth and seventeenth centuries, however, the mason burgesses endeavoured to prevent unfreemen from infringing their monopoly of trade. Thus in 1577, when wrights and masons had stopped certain unfree masons from build-

---

[1] *Laws*, 70, 71.   [2] *Ibid.*, 127.

[3] In the Burgh of Canongate, in July, 1630, the Incorporation of Wrights, Coopers and Masons fined a certain James Potter £3 for suffering an unfreeman to work in the liberty, but there is nothing in the Minute (Murray, 190) to indicate to which craft Potter belonged.

[4] See the section on Incorporations, p. 64 below.

[5] *Edinburgh, 1403–1528*, 31, 32.

ing, the municipality ordered that the said unfree masons, in accord with the Act of Parliament,[1] were to complete the said work and "commands this order to be kept in all times coming when wrights or masons become unreasonable in their prices".[2] In the seventeenth century, the hostility to unfreemen is shown in various minutes of the Lodge of Edinburgh.[3]

At Aberdeen a seal of cause, granted to the masons, wrights and coopers in 1527, was confirmed in 1541.[4] By the latter grant, it was provided that no man should be made a freeman of the said crafts until he had been examined by the deacons and found proficient, and that no one should be permitted to trade on his own account until he had been made free.

In Glasgow, where a seal of cause was granted to the masons and wrights in 1551,[5] no craftsman was entitled to work at his own hand without entering as a burgess and freeman;[6] but, according to a minute of the Incorporation dated 3 November, 1612, freemen could engage unfreemen to work for them, provided that the engagement was for a minimum period of a year.[7] In 1652, owing to the number of masons being insufficient as the result of a fire, the town council authorised the employment of any masons fit for the work, wherever they could be found.[8] In 1655, each stranger of the calling working for wages in the burgh was required to contribute 30s. Scots quarterly for the use of the poor of the craft.[9] In 1657, as a consequence of a petition of the deacons of the masons and wrights against the great employment given to strangers, the council ordered that no unfree mason or wright should take any further tasks or works in the burgh, beyond those he already had, and that in future masons and wrights from outside were only to work under freemen of the burgh.[10]

Co-operation among Masons.—Such evidence on the sub-

[1] Doubtless the Act of 1540 referred to above.
[2] *Edinburgh, 1573–89*, 58.   [3] Lyon, 26.
[4] Both the seals of cause are printed in Bain, 238–40.
[5] Cruikshank, 3 *folg.*   [6] *Ibid.*, 61.
[7] *Ibid.*, 62.   [8] *Glasgow, 1630–62*, 233.
[9] *Ibid.*, 323.   [10] *Ibid.*, 370.

ject of recruitment and mobility as we have examined, gives an indication of the extent to which masons worked in places outside their own areas, and also shows something of the attitude of the freeman masons of Edinburgh, Glasgow and Aberdeen towards the unfree masons who might seek work in their midst. It now remains to consider what voluntary co-operation, or compulsory collaboration, if any, of a more than local character, existed amongst masons in Scotland in the sixteenth and seventeenth centuries.

The chief examples of voluntary co-operation are afforded by the documents known as the St. Clair Charters of 1601 and 1628.[1] By the first, representatives of the Lodges of Edinburgh, St. Andrews, Haddington, Aitchison's Haven and Dunfermline, on behalf of the deacons, masters and freemen of the masons within the realm of Scotland, and with the assent of William Schaw, King's Master of Work, agreed that William St. Clair of Roslin should purchase from the King, for himself and his heirs, "liberty, freedom and jurisdiction" over all the masons in Scotland. The second charter, signed by representatives of the Lodges of Edinburgh, Dundee, Glasgow, Stirling, Dunfermline, Ayr and St. Andrews, on behalf of the deacons, masters and freemen of the masons and hammermen within the Kingdom of Scotland, is a confirmation and elaboration of the first charter. The interest of these charters lies not in the claims of the St. Clairs of Roslin to exercise a hereditary right of supervision over the masons of Scotland, a claim which appears to have been disallowed by the Court of the Exchequer in 1635,[2] but in the uniting of no fewer than five lodges in 1601, and of seven lodges in 1628, or of nine different lodges in all, from places more than eighty miles apart, to support that claim.

Of compulsory, or semi-compulsory, collaboration, more illustrations can be given. They mostly centre round the previously described office of Master of Work to the Crown of Scotland, an appointment which originally related to a particular work, such as Stirling Castle or Linlithgow Palace, but at a later date related, in some cases, to all royal

[1] Printed in Lyon, 65–8. [2] Lyon, 92–3.

works, in which case the holder was usually described as Principal Master of Work. The earliest of these wide appointments which we have been able to trace are those of Sir James Hammyltoun in 1539, of John Hammyltoune in 1543, and of Sir Robert Drummond in 1579. Better known among the King's Principal Masters of Work, either because of their greater administrative activities, or because their activities have been more fully recorded and preserved, are William Schaw, who apparently held office from the death of Sir Robert Drummond in 1592 [1] until his own death in 1602, and Sir Anthonie Alexander, who was appointed in 1630.

Three pieces of evidence relating to Schaw's period of office point to some kind of widespread collective activity amongst masons. (i) On 28 December, 1598, William Schaw promulgated, "with the consent of the masters after specified", what are known as the Schaw Statutes of 1598. Unfortunately, the names of the masters who consented do not appear to be specified in the copies which have survived, and thus we do not know from what lodges representatives attended. (ii) A year later, on 28 December, 1599, a further set of statutes and ordinances (directed more particularly to the Lodge of Kilwinning), was issued by William Schaw. It gave to that lodge certain supervisory powers over other lodges in the Nether Ward of Clydesdale, Glasgow, Ayr and Carrick. From the last clause, it would seem that the statutes were issued on the authority of the Warden General and Principal Master of Work, at the request of the Lodge of Kilwinning, but that certain privileges and powers which the lodge desired

---

[1] Schaw's writ of appointment is not recorded in the Privy Seal. We rely on Mylne ("Masters of Work to the Crown of Scotland", *Proc. Soc. Antiq. Scot.*, 1895–6, 49–68) for our dates for Schaw, as for all other details in this paragraph. Lyon, page 58, gives Schaw's date of appointment as 1583, based on an appendix to the 1848 edition of the *Laws and Constitutions of the Grand Lodge of Scotland*. Extracts from the Treasurer's Accounts are quoted (presumably from manuscripts in the Edinburgh Register House, the printed edition of the Accounts not being available for the dates in question) which show that William Schaw was Master of Work at Stirling Castle in 1585 and at Dunfermline in 1590, but it does not necessarily follow that he was Principal Master of Work at those dates.

could not be granted at the time, owing to the absence of the king from Edinburgh, and because no masters, other than the masters of the Lodge of Edinburgh, were present at the meeting in Edinburgh on December 27 and 28. This implies that for certain purposes a more representative gathering of masters was necessary than merely the masters of one lodge. Both on account of this implication, and because of the powers which the Lodge of Kilwinning exercised over other lodges in the West of Scotland, these statutes throw an interesting light on masonic collaboration. (iii) An entry in the Minute Book of the Lodge of Edinburgh, under date of 27 November, 1599,[1] records that a general meeting was to be held at St. Andrews on 13 January 1600, "for settling and taking order with the affairs of the lodge" which was to be attended by (a) two commissioners from "everie pircular ludge",[2] (b) by the whole of the masters and others within the jurisdiction of the Lodge of St. Andrews, and (c) by the Masters of Dundee and Perth, the penalty for failure to attend being £10 in each case. To judge by the context, the lodges represented by two commissioners were probably the individual subordinate lodges under the jurisdiction of the Lodge of St. Andrews, which, in that case, very possibly exercised some kind of supervision over Fifeshire lodges, corresponding to that exercised by the Lodge of Kilwinning over West of Scotland lodges. The "others within the jurisdiction of the Lodge of St. Andrews" were presumably the fellowcrafts and entered apprentices. As Dundee and Perth were mentioned separately by name, and were to be represented in a different manner from the other lodges, the presumption is that the lodges of Dundee and Perth were somewhat of the same standing as St. Andrews.

Another, and earlier, example of jurisdiction exercised over masons resident in a fairly wide area, is afforded by the election of Patrick Copeland of Udaught, by choice of a majority of the master masons of the district, to the office

---

[1] Extract printed in Lyon, 40.
[2] *Pircular* is presumably a misreading of p[tl]cular, i.e., *particular*. For the expression *euerie particular ludge*, meaning every single lodge, see the concluding words of the Schaw Statutes, 1598.

E

of Warden and Justice over the masons within the counties of Aberdeen, Banff and Kincardine.[1] This particular election was ratified by the King in 1590.

The most definite evidence of co-operation or collaboration to secure freedom of movement amongst masons is afforded by what are known as the Falkland Statutes of 1636,[2] which provided for the better regulation of masons, wrights and other artificers engaged in the building industry, by the formation of unprivileged companies outside those places where the trades in question were organised as privileged companies under seals of cause. The Statutes contemplated three types of case of masons working away from home: (a) masters and servants associated with a particular unprivileged company might work in the area of another unprivileged company on payment of certain fees; (b) artificers residing near a free burgh in which a privileged company was established by seal of cause, might be examined by such company and, if found proficient, might be admitted to the craft, in order that they might work outside their own area, in any unprivileged place, on payment of certain fees; (c) members of a privileged company and their servants might reside and work in any other company's bounds on payment of certain fees.[3]

---

[1] Lyon, 4, 5.

[2] These acts and statutes were promulgated at Falkland on 26 October, 1636, by Sir Anthonie Alexander, General Warden and Master of Work to His Majesty. A copy was entered in the book which ultimately became the second Minute Book of Aitchison's Haven Lodge (see Wallace-James, 34) and was subsequently accepted and approved by that Lodge; the Statutes and relevant entries from that Minute Book, now preserved in the archives of the Grand Lodge of Scotland, are printed in W. A. Laurie, *History of Freemasonry*, 2nd ed., 1859, 445–52. The Statutes are also printed in D. B. Morris, *The Incorporation of Mechanics of Stirling*. Copies were doubtless sent to other lodges for their information, but the only other copy which appears to have been preserved, and that only in part, is one entered in the Mark Book of the Lodge of Aberdeen, under the heading: "Laws and Statutes for Masons gathered out of their old writings by us who are the authors and subscribers of this book." We are greatly indebted to Bro. A. L. Miller, P.M. of the Lodge of Aberdeen, for kindly supplying us with a copy of the relevant parts of the Mark Book. The Aberdeen version consists of roughly the second half of the Aitchison's Haven version of the Statutes.

[3] For general discussion of the Falkland Statutes, see p. 68 below.

The Genesis of the Mason Word.—The existence, in the late sixteenth and early seventeenth centuries, of a considerable measure of co-operation and collaboration amongst masons in different parts of Scotland, such as is clearly indicated by the various cases to which we have drawn attention, made possible that widespread association among masons, without which the institution of the Mason Word could not have existed. That the various lodges scattered over Scotland should have communicated the same secret methods of recognition and should have kept touch with the changes and developments in those secrets, which almost certainly took place in the course of years, is really very remarkable. It would certainly not have been possible without close association amongst the interested parties, and probably not without some over-riding authority to control the whole institution. By what date such conditions had developed as would render feasible the introduction of the Mason Word, it is impossible to say. The Schaw Statutes of 1599 refer to the Lodge of Edinburgh as first and principal lodge in Scotland, and to the Lodge of Kilwinning as second lodge, in both cases "as of before"; but how long they had occupied such positions of responsibility there is no evidence to show. Nor do we know at what date there began that system of meetings of representatives of different lodges to discuss and decide matters of general interest to masons. Such meetings may have taken place several, or even many, years before those at the end of the sixteenth century, of which some knowledge has come down to us. Nor, in view of the previously mentioned scarcity of early Scottish records, can we be sure that Sir James Hammyltoun, appointed Principal Master of Work to the Crown in 1539, was the first holder of that office, the existence of which must have greatly facilitated, if it was not absolutely essential to, the establishment of the Mason Word.

On the other hand, it does not necessarily follow that the Mason Word as an institution was established as soon as conditions developed which rendered it possible. In so far as the Mason Word was part of the machinery for preventing unqualified masons or "cowans" from doing the work of qualified masons, it would hardly be established before the menace of unqualified masons became serious. Originally "cowan" meant a builder of drystone walls—it was only at some later, but unknown date, that it came to be applied derogatorily to one who did the work of a mason without having been regularly apprenticed or bred to the trade. That it was sometimes used in this sense by 1598 seems to follow from the injunction in the Schaw Statutes of 1598, which could hardly have been aimed at drystone wallers, that no master or fellowcraft was to employ cowans or send his servants to work with cowans, under penalty of £20 for each offence. How much earlier than 1598 the term was used in this sense we do not know.

Later,[1] it is pointed out that as the Mason Word was a privilege associated with the termination of an apprenticeship, or the admission to a fellowship, it might be as old as the system of apprenticeship, which can be traced at Cupar-Angus in 1466 and at Edinburgh in 1475. This was no doubt one factor governing the establishment of the institution of the Mason Word, but the other factors to which we have drawn attention above, viz., the need for some widespread association among masons to support the institution, and the menace of unqualified masons or "cowans" to stimulate the establishment of the institution, would seem even more important.

Among unqualified masons there might be not only (i) drystone wallers, or "cowans" in the original sense of the word, but (ii) masons who had not served a *lawful* apprenticeship and (iii) men who had served apprenticeships to masons, but had not been afterwards admitted "according to the manner and custom of making masons". Men of the second category are described as *loses* in *Melrose MS. No. 2*,[2] where the conditions making an apprenticeship lawful are defined. These approximated very closely to those regulating apprenticeships in the Schaw Statutes of 1598.[3] According to the *Melrose MS. No. 2*, masons were not to

---

[1] See p. 87.

[2] This version of the Old Charges, dated 1674, is printed in Vernon, *History of Freemasonry in Roxburghshire and Selkirkshire*, 58–63.

[3] Summarised on p. 45 above.

employ *loses* if properly qualified masons were available, and, if *loses* were employed, they were not to be allowed to know "the privilege of the compass, square, level and plumbrule". A mason of the third category is described as a *lewis* in *Dumfries MS. No. 3*,[1] where it is laid down that a mason or fellow "shall not make any mould, square or rule for any who is but a lewis."

Attention must be drawn to one further consideration. The Mason Word, in its original form, was presumably adopted by operative masons to serve some useful purpose. Little reflection is required in order to realise that it could have had little or no use merely as a means of distinguishing skilled masons from others. That could have been done better by means of a practical test, by requiring the man who claimed to be skilled to prove his ability on the spot by hewing or setting stones.[2] When, therefore, we find masons providing themselves with the Word, we may take it, probably, that they intended thereby to enable a man to demonstrate, not his skill, but his membership of some recognised group or association. A greater or lesser degree of skill was doubtless necessary in order to qualify for membership, but it was not the only qualification. Possession of the Mason Word implied that the man to whom it had been communicated accepted the rules, and shared in the privileges, of the body, legalised or other, which guarded it. The Mason Word, in short, was evidence not merely of a technical, but of a social or corporate qualification. In the next section, the various forms of organisation among masons will be examined, and it will be shown

---

[1] This version of the Old Charges, of the second half of the seventeenth century, is printed in Smith, *History of the Old Lodge of Dumfries*, 85–104. The following definition—"a lewis is such an one as hath served an apprenticeship to a mason but is not admitted afterwards according to this manner and custom of making masons"—also occurs in *Harris MS. No. 1* (*Freemasons' Chronicle*, Dec. 30, 1922) and *Harris MS. No. 2* (printed in *Quatuor Coronati Antigrapha*, iv), from the latter of which we quote. This definition is unknown to the *O.E.D.*, and is not one with which freemasons are familiar.

[2] That was apparently the practice at York Minster in 1370: "No mason shall be received at work . . . but he be first proved a week or more upon his well working" (Raine, *Fabric Rolls of York Minster* [Surtees Society], 181–2; Knoop and Jones, *The Mediaeval Mason*, 249).

that a particular type of lodge, which we describe as a "territorial lodge", imparted the Word to qualified members. It is known from surviving minute books and from the Schaw Statutes that such lodges existed in various places in Scotland by 1598 or 1599. How much earlier they existed, we know of no evidence to show.

5. ORGANISATION AMONG MASONS

(i) *Lodges.*—In the sixteenth and seventeenth centuries, the word "lodge" (luge, ludge) appears to have been used in Scotland in three different senses.

(*a*) It was used to designate a masons' workshop, such as was often specially erected in connection with a particular building operation. Thus in 1504, a house called *mason-luge*, near the gate of Falkland Palace, was purchased for £3 6s. 8d. for use in connection with work being under-taken there.[1] At the building of Dunkeld Bridge, expenses amounting to £6 12s. 7d. were incurred in 1513 "for building the masons' lodge"; in the same year, iron and timber for the *masonluge* were purchased at Linlithgow Palace.[2] The Accounts for works at Holyroodhouse in 1529–30 record expenditure "for wattles used for masons' lodges in the Abbey churchyard".[3] In the same accounts there are references in 1535–6 to the expenses incurred upon the masons' lodges, and to the thatching of the lodge.[4] At Edinburgh in 1555–6 various sums were spent "to mend the mason lodge that was decayed".[5] At Ayr in 1597–8, wrights were paid for putting up a house for the masons to hew in,[6] and it is doubtless this house which is referred to in the Accounts for 1599–1600 as the *masounis ludge.*[7] At the erection of the Tron Church, Edinburgh, in 1636, Thomas Young and his servants were paid for "making and building of four great lodges to the masons to hew in

---

[1] *Exch. R.,* xii, 205.   [2] *Treas. A/cs.,* iv, 524, 525.

[3] M.o.W. A/cs., i, under date 26 Feb. The lodges were presumably constructed of wattle and daub.

[4] *Ibid.,* v, f. 31.

[5] *Edinburgh, 1528–1557,* 364. This presumably refers to the lodge at St. Giles mentioned below.

[6] *Ayr,* 194.   [7] *Ibid.,* 203.

with a study (stoodie) at the end thereof for the master mason". In 1640, when the mason work in connection with the Parliament House, Edinburgh, was completed, the *ludge* was taken down.[1] In the contract of 1666, for the erection of Panmure House, Lord Panmure undertook to furnish "a good and sufficient *ludge* for the masons to hew their stone in, either in foul or fair weather".[2]

(*b*) "Lodge" was also used as the name of a permanent structure, serving amongst other purposes as a workshop for a more or less permanent staff of masons, governed by rules, either laid down, or approved, by their employers. In the *Council Register of Aberdeen* it is recorded that in 1483 the master of the Kirk work of St. Nicholas reported an agreement amongst "the masownys of the luge"[3] regarding their future conduct, the maximum penalty for a breach thereof being exclusion from the lodge.[4] Masons who in 1484, 1493 and 1498 were hired for a year by the Council to work at St. Nicholas, undertook in each case to render good service "in the luge and vteuche".[5] At St. Giles, Edinburgh, a statute made by the provost, dean of gild, baillies and council in 1491 lays down the conditions of employment of the master mason, his colleagues and servants, and includes a provision for "recreation in the common luge for half an hour" at four o'clock.[6] Thus, at Edinburgh, as at York, the masons' lodge, amongst other purposes, served as a place of refreshment for the masons during the afternoon break. Knowledge of the lodge at the Church of Our Lady, Dundee, is derived from the

[1] H. and W., 73.

[2] The use of the word *luge*, *ludge*, in Scotland to mean "masons' workshop" is identical with the use of the word *logia*, *logge*, in contemporary and older documents in England and on the continent.

[3] This expression appears to be the exact equivalent of "lathami de la loygge" which occurs in the Register of the Prior of Canterbury in 1429 (Bodl. Lib. Tanner MSS. 165).

[4] *Aberdeen*, i, 38, 39.

[5] *Ibid.*, 41–2, 52, 68 ; *vteuche*, "without," "outside of." See *O.E.D.* under *utouth*.

[6] *Edinburgh, 1403–1528*, 61, 62. This provision may be compared with a provision in the York Minster masons' ordinances of 1370 that "aftyr none yai may drynk in ye loge" (Raine, *Fabric Rolls of York Minster*, 181).

provisions of a contract of March 1537,[1] by which the provost, baillies and council of the burgh, together with the *Kirkmaister*, appointed George Boiss mason for life; in the conditions regulating the hours of work (discussed in an earlier section of this paper) reference is made to "the auld use and consuetude of Our Lady Luge of Dundee", and there can be little doubt that these, as well as other conditions of the contract, were but written statements of old established customs governing the employment of masons at that church.

The surviving records show that this type of permanent lodge was associated with a church fabric, although, owing to the close connection between town church and burgh administration in Scotland, the municipality apparently had an important share in approving the rules governing the masons employed in such lodges. Though we have noted such lodges only at St. Nicholas, Aberdeen, at St. Giles, Edinburgh, and Our Lady, Dundee, the likelihood is that similar lodges existed at other large churches in Scotland, although we have found no direct or indirect evidence of regulations governing such lodges.[2]

(c) "Lodge" also meant an organised body of masons associated with a particular town or district. The word appears to be used in this sense in the Schaw Statutes of 1598, where it is laid down "that there be a warden chosen in every year to have charge over every *ludge*", and in the Schaw Statutes of 1599, where it is provided "that Edinburgh shall be in all time coming as of before the first and principal *ludge* in Scotland and that Kilwinning be the second as before". In the section on Co-operation among Masons we have mentioned, in addition to Edinburgh and Kilwinning, the Lodges of Dundee, St. Andrews, Perth, Dunfermline, Aitchison's Haven, Glasgow, Stirling and Ayr, all of which were "territorial lodges", if, for want of a better term, we may so describe this type of lodge. These "territorial lodges" were doubtless mostly concerned with

[1] Printed in Mylne, 63, 64.

[2] In England, lodges of this type undoubtedly existed at York, for which lodge three sets of masons' ordinances are extant, and at Durham and Hereford Cathedrals, for which contracts appointing masons have survived.

particular burghs, though that was not so in all cases, as is shown by the location of a lodge at Kilwinning, which was not a burgh. The Lodge of Aitchison's Haven met not only at the Haven, but at Fisherrow, Musselburgh, Inversk, Prestonpans and Dalkeith,[1] all places in Midlothian or Haddingtonshire a few miles east or south-east of Edinburgh. Of these places, only Musselburgh was a burgh.

The main functions of a "territorial lodge"[2] appear to have been to discharge certain official or semi-official duties of a trade character, such as regulating the terms of apprenticeship, keeping records of the reception and entry of apprentices and the admission of fellowcrafts, and assigning "marks" to members of the lodge. Other rules concerned masters more particularly, such as not taking work over another master's head, not employing the apprentice or journeyman of another mason, and not employing cowans, or causing his servants to work with them. The lodge also concerned itself with the settlement of disputes between masters and their servants. In addition, it collected funds, by way both of fees and fines, for pious uses and for the relief of distress among members, and indulged in a certain amount of feasting at the expense of candidates. Finally, it conferred the benefit of the Mason Word on qualified members.

Whilst there was only one "territorial lodge" in any one place,[3] there might well be, in addition, "lodges" in one

---

[1] Wallace-James, 30, 32.

[2] We rely on three sources: (i) the Schaw Statutes of 1598 and 1599; (ii) the Mutual Agreement of 1658 of the Lodge of Scoon and Perth (D. Crawford Smith, *History of the Lodge of Scoon and Perth*, 45–7); the Laws and Statutes of 1670 of the Lodge of Aberdeen (Miller, 57–65); the Mutual Agreement of 1675 of the Lodge of Melrose (W. F. Vernon, *History of Freemasonry in Roxburghshire and Selkirkshire*, 13, 14); and some Regulations of 1687 of the Old Lodge of Dumfries (J. Smith, *History of the Old Lodge of Dumfries*, 9, 10), which are surviving examples of seventeenth-century lodge rules; (iii) the early minutes of the Lodges of Aitchison's Haven and of Edinburgh, the former commencing in 1598 and the latter in 1599 (Wallace-James; Lyon).

[3] The apparent anomaly of the existence in Edinburgh of the Lodge of Canongate Kilwinning, established in 1677, in addition to the Lodge of Edinburgh (Mary's Chapel) is accounted for by the fact that Canongate was outside the Edinburgh boundary at that period.

or both of the other senses. Thus in Edinburgh in 1636, the four lodges, previously mentioned as being erected in connection with the building of the Tron Church, were clearly distinct from the Lodge of Edinburgh, and the same was true of the Lodge of St. Giles, if it still existed at that date.[1]

(ii) *Incorporations.*—These bodies existed in certain burghs for ruling and governing particular crafts, and for furthering divine service among their members. They were established by what are known as seals of cause, which, in some cases at least, were rules and statutes made by the craftsmen and approved by the municipality.[2] In those cases where the masons belonged to an incorporated trade, they were generally associated with the wrights, and possibly also with other building crafts.

Our information concerning incorporations of masons is unfortunately but slight. We can trace only six before the end of the seventeenth century: Edinburgh, where the masons and wrights obtained a seal of cause from the municipality in 1475;[3] Aberdeen, where a seal of cause was granted by the burgh to the coopers, wrights and masons in 1527 and ratified in 1541, when the carvers, slaters and painters were added to the Incorporation;[4] Glasgow, where the organisation dates from 1551;[5] Canongate, where the Minutes of the Incorporation of the Wrights, Coopers and Masons from 1630, and the names of the deacons and the admissions from 1585, have survived;[6] Lanark, where a

---

[1] In England, so far as we are aware, there were no "territorial lodges"; the only bodies of masons discharging official or semi-official functions were described as "companies" or "fellowships"; consequently the word "lodge" does not occur in England in this sense in the sixteenth and seventeenth centuries.

[2] *Edinburgh, 1403–1528*, 31–2.

[3] *Ibid.*, 31–2. The trade of the coopers was added in 1489; the grants were ratified by the Archbishop of St. Andrews in 1517, and confirmed by charter from James V in 1527 (J. Colston, *The Incorporated Trades of Edinburgh*, 65).

[4] The seals of cause are printed in Bain, 238–40.

[5] Seal of cause printed in Cruikshank, 3–6. It included the masons, coopers, slaters and quarriers, and several other trades, of which the wrights were almost certainly one. There is a doubt because some words in the document are illegible.

[6] Murray, 187.

new seal of cause was granted to the masons and wrights in 1674;[1] and Ayr, where an Incorporation of Masons and Wrights, known as the Squaremen Incorporation, apparently obtained its charter in 1556. Its deacon was one of the signatories of the St. Clair charter of 1628; its statutes are said to have been revised in 1660.[2] It is quite likely that incorporations of masons and wrights existed in other burghs in the seventeenth century, but we have failed to trace them in such printed records as we have examined.[3]

Amongst the trade functions discharged by incorporations of masons [4] were some which were very similar to those discharged by masons' lodges, as for example, the control of apprentices and servants, and the regulation of masters. In addition, the incorporations were also responsible for conducting periodic searches to see that the work done was "sufficient and good", or "loyally and truly done to all builders". The officers of the incorporations were also to examine, by an essay of craft, any person wishing to work at the trade, in order to ascertain if he was qualified. Further, in some cases at least, it was provided that no craftsman was to be allowed to work on his own account until he had been admitted a burgess and freeman. Thus an incorporation, like a craft gild, afforded some protection to the public by seeing that work was properly done and that the craftsmen were properly qualified. On the other

[1] *Lanark*, 195–6. The former charter, of unstated date, had become illegible as a result of cleaning, its holder having died of plague in 1645.

[2] Lyon, 249, 68, 131.

[3] At Perth the Incorporation of Wrights included the masons (W. Harvey, *Ancient Stirling Ludge*, 22); at Dundee, wrights, masons and slaters were combined in a body known as "The Three Trades" (*ibid.*, 22), but we do not know at what dates these organisations were established. At Stirling, the masons in the first part of the seventeenth century belonged to the Omnium Gatherum, and in the second half to the Mechanics, a "tolerated community", i.e., an organised community which had not been incorporated by a seal of cause (*ibid.*, 22 and D. B. Morris, *The Incorporation of Mechanics of Stirling*, 4). At Dumfries, there appears to have been an Incorporation of Masons in the early eighteenth century (J. Smith, *History of the Old Lodge of Dumfries*, 18).

[4] We rely on the various seals of cause, and the extracts from books of the Incorporations of Edinburgh and Glasgow, quoted by Lyon and Cruikshank.

hand, it protected the master tradesman from the competition of masters who were not free of the particular burgh.

It may, further, be noted that masons, like other craftsmen, were able, through their craft organisations, to take a part in civic government. An Act of 1469 [1] provided that in the royal burghs each craft should, through one of its members, have a voice in the election of municipal officers. In Edinburgh, where there were fourteen main crafts, the municipal council in the seventeenth century included fourteen deacons; but of these only six were full members. They were called "council deacons" or "ordinary deacons", and the other eight "extraordinary deacons". The distinction was based on an order of the council in 1569, excluding from membership the crafts concerned with provision of sustenance, which apparently included housing; the same order also excluded cordwainers and others "of sic rude occupatioun". Thus James Hamiltoun, mason, in 1641–2, John Mylne in 1642–3 and 1643–4, and Robert Prestoun, mason, in 1644–5, were extraordinary deacons.[2] In September 1648, however, the furriers, wrights, masons, bakers, fleshers, websters, waulkers and bonnet makers protested against the monopolising, by the other six crafts, of the choice of the six council deacons, and demanded that those members should be chosen from the fourteen crafts "without respect of ane craft more than another",[3] in accord with a decree arbitral of 1583. The council agreed to the petition and ordered the observance of the judgment of 1583. Accordingly, it became possible for members of the hitherto excluded crafts to be full members of the council. David Thomson, wright, was so in 1649–50 [4] and John Milne, mason, in 1653–4.[5]

Reference must still be made to two problems about which our curiosity is aroused, but cannot, unfortunately, be fully satisfied, namely, the manner in which the masons co-operated with the wrights and other crafts within their

---

[1] *Laws*, 32. [2] *Edinburgh*, 1642–55, 1, 13, 35, 53.
[3] *Ibid.*, 169. [4] *Ibid.*, 213.
[5] *Ibid.*, 323. He was a member of the council, but not as a representative of the crafts, in 1655–6 (*ibid.*, 387), by which time he was probably of too great consequence to be regarded as a mere craftsman.

incorporation, and the relations which existed between an incorporation of masons and a lodge of masons in the same town. Regarding the first problem, the only definite evidence we have relates to Glasgow, where in 1600 the wrights complained of the inconvenience of masons judging wrights' work and wrights judging masons' work. As a consequence, the wrights—including glazing wrights, boat wrights, painters, bowyers and sawyers—were separated from the masons and given articles of their own,[1] it being especially stipulated, however, that these new articles were not to prejudice artificers who undertook both wrights' work and masons' work.[2] At Edinburgh, the masons remained united with the wrights in the Incorporation of Mary's Chapel; possibly the Incorporation left the bulk of the business affecting masons to the Lodge, the government of which, in this particular case, appears to have been vested in the master masons who were members of the Incorporation.[3] That the Lodge should be controlled in this way probably supplies one solution of our second problem; during the seventeenth century, the deacon, or chief officer of the masons in the Incorporation of Mary's Chapel, appears largely to have directed the Lodge,[4] so that no clash between Incorporation and Lodge was very likely to occur.[5] At Glasgow, an old minute book (1600–81) of the Incorporation of Masons has survived, but no early records of the Lodge, so that we can obtain little information about the relation of the two bodies. A perusal of the extracts from the minute book printed in Cruikshank does, however, suggest that the Incorporation kept a firm hand over the Lodge; on one occasion, the Incorporation appears to have ordered the warden of the Lodge to enter the son of the deacon as an apprentice in the Lodge; at all times, the Incorporation seems to have dealt in considerable detail

---

[1] *Charters and Documents relating to the City of Glasgow, 1175–1649*, 43–4.
[2] *Ibid.*, clxxxv.   [3] Lyon, 42.   [4] *Ibid.*, 220.
[5] In the early eighteenth century, the journeyman members rebelled against the oligarchical control of the Lodge of Edinburgh, and formed a lodge of their own, the Lodge of Journeymen Masons, but this has no bearing on the relation between the Lodge and the Incorporation (*ibid.*, 143 *folg.*; J. S. Seggie and D. L. Turnbull, *Annals of the Lodge of Journeymen Masons, No. 8*, Chap. I).

with problems affecting apprentices and servants, actually requiring that all apprentices' indentures should be prepared by the clerk to the Incorporation, to whom certain fees were also payable for booking freeman-apprentices and servants. The Incorporation also took steps to prevent masons working with cowans, and concerned itself with the settlement of disputes amongst masons. Thus at Glasgow, the Incorporation appears to have attended to various matters which elsewhere were managed by the lodge.

In Canongate, the Incorporation appears to have been much older than the Lodge (Canongate Kilwinning), which was not established until 1677, when the Lodge of Kilwinning gave certain masons of Canongate power to enter, receive, and pass qualified persons on behalf of the Lodge of Kilwinning.[1] The earliest surviving minutes of the Canongate Lodge date from 1735.[2] A. A. A. Murray implies that it began as a purely speculative lodge,[3] but produces no evidence to support such a conclusion. Very clear evidence would be necessary to prove that the daughter lodge discharged functions entirely different from those of the mother lodge, which, so far as we are aware, was purely operative in the seventeenth century.

(iii) *Privileged and Unprivileged Companies.*—The Falkland Statutes of 1636[4] provided for the establishment of companies of masons, wrights and other artificers engaged in building, in all convenient places in the Kingdom of Scotland where no companies established by seals of cause already existed. These latter companies, which existed in certain free burghs, are referred to in the Statutes as "privileged companies", and the new ones, to be set up under the Statutes, as "unprivileged companies". The term "privileged company" would seem to be another name for the incorporations which we examined in the previous section. The term "unprivileged company" very probably corresponds more or less to the expression "tolerated community", which has been used to describe the organisation of the Mechanics at Stirling, to which the masons belonged in the later part of the seventeenth century, an organisa-

---

[1] A. Mackenzie, *History of the Lodge Canongate Kilwinning, No. 2*, 12.

[2] *Ibid.*, 28.   [3] *A.Q.C.*, xxi, 187.   [4] See note 2 on page 56 above.

tion at that period with a lower status than that of an incorporation.[1]

An "unprivileged company" was to examine artificers and to admit those who were found qualified to be masters of their respective arts and crafts, provided they had served a proper apprenticeship. These masters were to elect each year a deacon or warden, and a box-master, to manage the affairs of the company. The Statutes regulated the number and duration of apprenticeships, the booking of apprentices and servants, the mutual relations of masters, the method of settling disputes, and the fees to be paid in various connections, all very much along the lines followed by the incorporations. The Statutes further made provision for co-operation among the various companies, and laid down the conditions on which the members of privileged and unprivileged companies could work outside their own areas, matters to which we referred in an earlier section on Co-operation among Masons. Lastly, they stipulated that no unadmitted person was to take any work in hand, or to take apprentices or servants, until he had been admitted a master in a company.

The Falkland Statutes of 1636 become significant when related not merely to the history of Scottish masonry, but also to the trends which, to a greater or lesser degree, may be observed in several European countries during the phase of transition from early to modern economic organisation. Mediaeval industrial organisation was predominantly local; a craft gild in each town normally controlled, under the municipal authorities, the particular trade of the baker or the smith within that town. A variety of factors, and especially the expansion of industry, with production not merely for local and immediate needs but for more distant and for future consumption, tended to bring about the breakdown of the old order in more ways than one. The gilds, especially in England, declined; and industries, both in England and France, tended to move out of the towns to the country, where labour and provisions were cheaper, and where restrictions on production were less enforceable. Since nobody in those days normally adopted a laissez-faire

---

[1] W. Harvey, *op. cit.*, 22, 23.

attitude, it followed that the State was obviously the authority which must be concerned with the functions no longer adequately discharged by local gilds. Thus the State in England, by the Statute of Artificers, 1563, sought to generalise the old gild institution of apprenticeship, to maintain standards of workmanship and to provide for fixing hours of work and rates of wages. In France, where the gilds, though full of abuses, had more vitality than in England, Colbert, carrying on with new energy an old policy, attempted by edicts of 1673, 1674 and 1675, to force gild organisation on all the crafts, and at the same time to strengthen a centralised control of gild organisation.[1]

Similar ideas and policies can be traced elsewhere, e.g., in eighteenth-century Würtemberg. One point in the organisation there enforced is of special interest in connection with the Falkland Statutes; that is the establishment of *Landeszünften*,[2] gilds whose membership was not confined to one town but was scattered in several places. If in any locality there were not enough men of one trade to form a gild (*Zunft*), the craftsmen who carried on that trade were incorporated in an association having its headquarters in the nearest important town. There were, e.g., two incorporations of locksmiths, with headquarters respectively at Stuttgart and Tübingen. Such headquarters were called *Hauptlade*, from the chest (or, as the Falkland Statutes call it, the box) in which the funds and documents of the gild were kept. There existed at one time a difference between *Hauptlade* and *Nebenlade*, or chief and local headquarters, which would not have seemed strange to Scotsmen familiar with Mother Kilwinning and its subordinate lodges.

We may note further, as throwing some light on the Falkland Statutes, a difference of importance in France between the *métier libre* and the *métier juré*, or *jurande*, that is, between the "free" and the incorporated mystery. The former was by no means without customs or regulations,[3] but it had not the same status as the latter. French policy

---

[1] Henri Sée, *L'Évolution Commerciale et Industrielle de la France sous l'Ancien Régime*, 84–6.

[2] Otto, *Das deutsche Handwerk*, 71–2.   [3] Henri Sée, *op. cit.*, 56.

moved as it were between two forces. Colbert desired to force the free crafts to become incorporations; but, on the other hand, though some crafts were willing to be incorporated, the municipal authorities and the existing incorporations, jealous of their status, were opposed to such a development.[1] We take the unprivileged companies of the Falkland Statutes to be something like the *métier libre* of France, and the privileged companies to be broadly equivalent to the *métier juré*, that is incorporations set up by burghal authority (delegated from the Crown) by means of a seal of cause.

If these considerations be borne in mind, the policy underlying the Falkland Statutes will become clearer. There is no reason to suppose that the framers were consciously influenced by English or continental measures; but they arrived, by similar means, at a programme calculated to meet the special needs and conditions of the building industry in Scotland. There, as elsewhere, much building had to be done outside the towns, but full gild organisation was confined, as has been shown, to a few places; there was, consequently, a danger of insufficiently qualified artisans being employed, to the damage of the public interest; and also of the interests of masters of crafts suffering by defect of organisation. To secure adequate skill, therefore, the Falkland Statutes attempt, like the Statute of Artificers, to make apprenticeship general; they rely for the purpose, however, not on Justices of the Peace, as in England, but on the extension of gild organisation, as in France and Würtemberg. In order, probably, not to antagonise the existing incorporations, the Falkland Statutes leave their privileges undiminished, and attempt to set up new organisations (or perhaps to legitimise existing ones) elsewhere. It is noteworthy that, as in France, some centralised control of the companies is contemplated; for their chief officers are to be accountable to the General Warden, a royal official, who is also to collect half the amounts of fines imposed for breaches of the regulations. Participation in fines was at one time the practice in France,[2] and, apart altogether

[1] Henri Sée, *op. cit.*, 53–4.
[2] H. Hauser, *Ouvriers du Temps Passé* (1927), 9.

from the good of industry, was one of the motives of royal interference in gild organisation.

There is little evidence to show to what extent "unprivileged companies" were established in Scotland under the provisions of the Falkland Statutes. It would, however, appear that in 1637 there existed in Stirling a body, including wrights and masons, which formally accepted those statutes, and that in 1638 the General Warden and King's Master of Works appointed its deacon and warden.[1]

COMPARISON OF SCOTTISH AND ENGLISH CONDITIONS

In most sections of this paper, we have drawn attention to marked resemblances or differences between Scottish and English conditions, though we have done so very briefly, and frequently without even giving references, as we have written at length about English conditions elsewhere.[2] The resemblances are hardly surprising, as the organisation of the building industry was very similar in all countries of Western Europe in the Middle Ages.[3] The main differ-

---

[1] See the documents quoted in David B. Morris, "The Incorporation of Mechanics of Stirling" (*Stirling Arch. Soc.*, Oct. 1930), 11.

[2] A detailed picture of the conditions under which the English mason worked and lived in the Middle Ages and early modern times (with full references) will be found in our book, *The Mediaeval Mason* (Manchester University Press, 1933) and in the following subsequent papers of ours: "Some Notes on Three Early Documents relating to Masons" (*A.Q.C.*, xliv), ' Henry Yevele and his Associates" (*R.I.B.A. Journal*, May, 1935); "The London Mason in the Seventeenth Century" (*A.Q.C.*, xlviii); "The Rise of the Mason Contractor" (*R.I.B.A. Journal*, Oct. 1936); "The Impressment of Masons for Windsor Castle" (*Economic History*, Feb. 1937); "The Impressment of Masons in the Middle Ages" *Economic History Review*, Nov. 1937); "The Bolsover Castle Building Account, 1613" (issued in advance of *A.Q.C.*, xlix); "The Decline of the Mason-Architect in England" (*R.I.B.A. Journal*, Sept. 1937); "The Sixteenth Century Mason" (issued in advance of *A.Q.C.*, l); "Overtime in the Age of Henry VIII" (*Economic History*, Feb. 1938); "The English Medieval Quarry" (*Economic History Review*, Nov. 1938); "The London Masons' Company" (*Economic History*, Feb. 1939). Biographical details concerning a score of English mediaeval masons will be found in the Appendix to our *Introduction to Freemasonry* (Manchester University Press, 1937) and in our "Notes on Three Mediaeval Master Masons" (*Misc. Lat.*, Nov. 1937).

[3] See our chapter on the Mediaeval Building Industry in vol. 2 of the forthcoming *Cambridge Economic History*.

ences are primarily due, in our opinion, to geological factors, and not, as some might be inclined to suppose, to the absence of close relations between the two countries, or to the strength of French influence in Scotland, from the time of the Scottish Wars of Independence in the fourteenth century, until the union of the two crowns in the early seventeenth century.[1]

The best building stones are magnesian and oolitic limestones, such as the magnesian limestones of Yorkshire (e.g. Huddlestone and Thevesdale), and the oolitic limestones of Somerset (e.g., Bath and Doulting), Oxfordshire (e.g., Taynton and Burford), Dorset (e.g., Portland), Northants (e.g., Barnack), Rutland (e.g., Ketton), Lincolnshire (e.g., Ancaster); and also the celebrated Caen stone of Normandy which is closely allied to the English oolites. These fine and evenly grained stones constitute the best qualities of "freestone", that is, stone which can be freely worked in any direction and which, consequently, is especially adapted for carving and undercutting. The point to which we would draw particular attention is that there are no magnesian or oolitic limestones in Scotland,[2] most of the rocks belonging to older geological formations. Some of the calciferous Scottish sandstone, more especially that known as "Hailes sandstone", quarried near Edinburgh, is "freestone", though not of the highest grade. The Coal Measures of Lanarkshire, as well as Old Red Sandstone found in the basins of the Forth and Clyde, and in other parts of Scotland, yield useful building stone, though not suitable for carving or undercutting, and the same is true of the granites, more especially associated with the name of Aberdeen.

[1] The cultural and social break between the two countries was probably not so great as is sometimes suggested. As Dr. Coulton has pointed out in his *Scottish Abbeys and Social Life* (pp. 33–4), "all through the Middle Ages there was less difference between Yorkshire or Northumberland and Lothian or Fife, than between both of them and Kent. . . . In literature, indeed, this bond was not broken even by the Wars of Independence; and the Scottish Chaucerians were better followers of their master than any Englishman was." Or again (p. 36), "England had enormous influence on mediaeval Scottish culture through her monastic colonies."

[2] See J. Watson, *British and Foreign Building Stones, passim.*

THE SCOTTISH MASON

This dearth in Scotland of "freestone" in general, and of the best qualities in particular, had a very important influence on conditions in the Scottish building industry. First, it probably accounts for the fact that the word "freemason", i.e., freestone mason, was unknown in Scotland as a trade designation; secondly, it helps to explain why there was comparatively little differentiation between the various classes of mason in Scotland; thirdly, it doubtless constitutes an important reason why Scotland developed architectural styles of its own, characterised in general by simplicity and austerity, apart from its turrets, and an absence of elaborate decorated work, gargoyles and the like; fourthly, it would explain a possible lack in Scotland of large quarry undertakings comparable with various important English mediaeval quarries,[1] or with the great quarries of Caen, which in each case supplied their high-grade stone to distant building operations, notwithstanding the heavy costs of carriage.

As stone capable of being used for building, though not necessarily high-class building stone, was found easily accessible over a wide area in Scotland, the erection of buildings of local stone in place of structures mainly of timber, became fairly common in the sixteenth and seventeenth centuries, and stone workers, prepared to win, dress and lay stone, were probably to be found in most burghs, and even in country districts. The quality of work done by some of these men, who had received little or no systematic training, was doubtless low, and it was from this type of worker, probably, that the "cowans" were recruited. The erection of numerous small stone buildings over a wide area favoured the growth of small master tradesmen employing one or two servants; thus the system of independent craftsmen or "little masters" appears to have flourished in Scotland in the sixteenth and seventeenth centuries, though at an earlier period monastic buildings had doubtless been erected, as in England, on the direct labour system, organised by monastic officials, and supported by the financial resources of the Church; a similar procedure had doubtless

[1] See our paper "The English Medieval Quarry", *Economic History Review*, Nov. 1938.

been adopted in the case of the early stone castles erected by the Crown. Connected with the system of independent craftsmen or "little masters," there tended to grow up, either spontaneously, or possibly as the result of official encouragement, local organisations of masons to watch over their interests, the "lodges"—the "territorial lodges" as we have called them—which existed not only in the larger burghs, but also in the smaller burghs, and occasionally in country districts. Thus the "territorial lodge", the "cowan", and the "Mason Word" (to help to protect members of lodges from cowans), all sprang from special features of the Scottish building industry, due directly or indirectly to the dearth of freestone in Scotland and to the widespread availability of local stone capable of being used for building. We have already discussed the subjects of the "cowan" and the "lodge"; in the study which follows, an attempt is made to examine the "Mason Word" as an operative institution, and to trace its influence on the Freemasonry of to-day.

THE MASON WORD

THE MASON WORD

The Mason Word more than a mere word. The *Edinburgh Register House MS.*, endorsed "Some questions anent the mason word 1696," shows that there were two distinct ceremonies. Entered Apprentices and their secrets. Relative age of the two ceremonies. The Five Points of Fellowship in relation to the Noah story in the *Graham MS.* (1726) and the Hiram story in Prichard's *Masonry Dissected* (1730). The possible origin of these stories. The *Sloane MS.*, 3329 (*c.* 1700), a tract headed: "A Narrative of the Freemasons word and signes." The possibility that the various MSS. indirectly reveal THE Mason Word. The age of the Mason Word as an institution. The *Trinity College, Dublin MS.* (1711) as a link between operative and speculative masonry. Influence exercised by the Mason Word on the development of masonic ceremonies.

THE subject which I have chosen for my Prestonian Lecture is the Mason Word, and the customs and usages associated with its communication, about which all too little is at present known. What little is known, however, suggests that this operative forerunner of our speculative rites probably throws more light on the origins of our present ceremonies than do those early Craft regulations and mediaeval histories of masonry, commonly known as the MS. *Constitutions of Masonry*, or, more familiarly, as the Old Charges. The MS. *Constitutions* present a wider field for investigation, as approximately one hundred different versions of them, ranging in date from the late fourteenth to the early nineteenth century, are known, and they have naturally been studied in considerable detail.[1] My field to-night is much narrower, as the principal materials on which I rely for my study of the Mason Word consist only of five late seventeenth- or early eighteenth-century manuscripts. Two of these,

[1] See, e.g., Hughan, *Old Charges of British Freemasons*, 1st ed., 1872; rev. 2nd ed., 1895; Gould, *Commentary on the Regius Poem, Q.C.A.*, i (1889); Speth, *Commentary on the Cooke MS., Q.C.A.*, ii (1890); Poole, *The Old Charges*, 1924; *The Old Charges in Eighteenth Century Masonry*, Prestonian Lecture for 1933; Poole and Worts, *The "Yorkshire" Old Charges of Masons*, 1935; Knoop, Jones and Hamer, *The Two Earliest Masonic MSS.* [the *Regius* and *Cooke* MSS.], 1938.

the *Edinburgh Register House MS.* (1696) and the *Chetwode Crawley MS.* (*c.* 1700),[1] are practically identical, apart from verbal variations and points of spelling and punctuation, with the all-important exception that the former is endorsed with a date. Thus the information is mainly derived from four documents, the *Edinburgh Register House MS.* (1696), the *Graham MS.* (1726), the *Trinity College, Dublin MS.* (1711), and the *Sloane MS.* 3329 (*c.* 1700). The last has been known for many years,[2] but its importance has recently been greatly enhanced by the discovery of the first two. Jointly, these MSS. constitute a most valuable source of information about early masonic ceremonies, and I am glad to avail myself of the opportunity afforded by my appointment as Prestonian Lecturer, to draw the attention of the Brethren to some of the significance of these four documents.

At the outset, I desire to acknowledge my indebtedness to various masonic students, and especially to Bro. the Rev. Herbert Poole, who has made such a close study of the Old Charges and of contemporary Masonic MSS.[3] It was his recent paper on the *Graham MS.* which first caused me to turn my attention to the various MSS. forming the basis of this lecture.

THE MASON WORD MORE THAN A MERE WORD

The justification for stressing the importance of the Mason Word as a factor in the development of masonic ceremonies, lies in the fact that it consisted of something substantially more than a mere word. Thus the Rev.

[1] Discovered at the beginning of the century [Hughan, *A.Q.C.*, xvii (1904), 91, 92], this MS. is now in the possession of the Grand Lodge of Ireland. A transcript appears in the Masonic Reprints of the Lodge of Research, No. 2429, Leicester. Its contents have subsequently proved to be practically the same as those of the *Edinburgh Register House MS.*, except that the two parts are transposed.

[2] It is quoted in the English edition of Findel's *History of Freemasonry*, published in 1865.

[3] See more especially "Masonic Ritual and Secrets before 1717," *A.Q.C.*, xxxvii (1924); and "The Graham Manuscript," *A.Q.C.*, l (1937).

I enjoy one definite advantage over earlier writers approaching the same problem: thanks to the recent discovery of the *Edinburgh Register House MS.*, endorsed 1696, I have escaped their difficulties regarding the probable dates

Robert Kirk, Minister of Aberfoyle, writing in 1691,[1] says the Mason Word "is like a Rabbinical Tradition, in way of comment on Jachin and Boaz, the two Pillars erected in Solomon's Temple (I Kings, 7, 21), with ane Addition of some secret Signe delyvered from Hand to Hand, by which they know and become familiar one with another." A letter of 1697 states that "The Laird[s] of Roslin . . . are obliged to receive the mason's word which is a secret signall masons have thro' out the world to know one another by. They alledge 'tis as old as since Babel, when they could not understand one another and they conversed by signs. Others would have it no older than Solomon. However it is, he that hath it will bring his brother mason to him without calling to him or your perceiving of the signe."[2]

THE *EDINBURGH REGISTER HOUSE MS.*

The *Edinburgh Register House MS.*,[3] a document discovered about 1930 among the records in the Historical Department of the Register House, Edinburgh, is considerably more informative. It is endorsed "Some Questiones Anent the mason word 1696" and consists of two parts, the first headed "Some Questiones That Masons use to put to those who have ye word before they will acknowledge them," and the second "The forme of giveing the mason word."

of the *Sloane* and *Chetwode Crawley MSS.* The handwriting of these two MSS. points to *circa* 1700; so does the fact that the *Chetwode Crawley MS.* contains, almost verbatim, the words of the so-called "Haughfoot Minute" of 1702 (Poole, *A.Q.C.*, xxxvii, 7). The MSS., however, refer to two ceremonies, whereas many masonic students maintained that there was only one prior to 1723. This conflict of external and internal evidence led to much doubt about the probable dates. Now that we know for certain that there were two distinct ceremonies at least as early as 1696, there need be no hesitation in accepting 1700 as the approximate date of these two MSS.

[1] *The Secret Commonwealth of Elves, Fauns and Fairies*, 3rd ed., 1933, 108.

[2] *Hist. MSS. Com., Portland MSS.*, ii, 56. For particulars about the Lairds of Roslin, a branch of the St. Clair family, and their claim to be protectors and patrons of the Craft in Scotland, see Murray Lyon, *History of the Lodge of Edinburgh (Mary's Chapel), No.* 1, Tercentenary Edition, 64–72.

[3] Edinburgh Register House, Miscellaneous Papers, No. 52. A photographic reproduction appears in *A.Q.C.*, xliii (1930), 153–5, and a transcript in the *Trans. of the Manchester Assoc. for Masonic Research*, xxii (1932), 143, in each case with an introduction by Bro. J. Mason Allan.

The test questions relate partly to the conditions of admittance, and partly to matters with which nobody could be acquainted without previous instruction. As the MS. provides answers to all the questions, and states that they have to be answered exactly, it is obvious that the necessary instruction regarding all the questions must have been given to a candidate either at his admission or subsequently.

As the questions and answers are not very long, I propose to read them in full,[1] in order to give the Brethren a first-hand acquaintance with the kind of Examination to be found in all the manuscripts with which we have to deal:

Q. 1: Are you a mason? *Ans:* Yes.

Q. 2: How shall I know it? *Ans:* You shall know it in time and place convenient. *Remark the fors[ai]d answer is only to be made when there is company present who are not masons. But if there be no such company by, you should answer by* signes, tokens and other points of my entrie.

Q. 3: What is the first point? *Ans:* Tell me the first point ile tell you the second. The first is to heill[2] and conceall; second, under no less pain, which is then cutting of your throat. *For you most make that sign when you say that.*

Q. 4: Where wes you entered? *Ans:* At the honourable lodge.

Q. 5: What makes a true and perfect lodge? *Ans:* seven masters, five entered apprentices, A dayes journey from a burroughs town, without bark of dog or crow of cock.[3]

---

[1] To facilitate reading, the various abbreviations used in the MS. for "question" and "answer" have been made uniform, the punctuation has been modernized, and such sentences as appear to be instructions have been printed in italics.

[2] *Heill, hele, heal:* to hide, conceal, to keep secret (O.E.D.).

[3] Cf. Laws and Statutes of the Lodge of Aberdeen, 1670, rule iii, "that no lodge be holden within a dwelling house wher ther is people living in it but in the open fieldes except it be ill weather, and then Let ther be a house chosen that no person shall heir nor sie ws"; and rule v., "that all entering prentises be entered in our antient outfeild Lodge in the mearnes in the parish of negg at the sconces at the poynt of the ness" (Miller, *Notes on the Early History and Records of the Lodge, Aberdeen,* 59, 63).

Q. 6: Does no less make a true and perfect lodge?
Ans: Yes, five masons and three entered apprentices, &c.

Q. 7: Does no less? *Ans:* The more the merrier, the fewer the better chear.

Q. 8: What is the name of your lodge? *Ans:* Kilwinning.

Q. 9: How stands your lodge? *Ans:* east and west as the temple of jerusalem.

Q. 10: where wes the first lodge? *Ans:* in the porch of Solomon's Temple.

Q. 11: Are there any lights in your lodge? *Ans:* yes, three—the north east, s w, and eastern passage. The one denotes the maste[r] mason, the other the warden. The third the setter croft.

Q. 12: Are there any jewells in your lodge? *Ans:* Yes three—Perpend [1] Esler [ashlar], a square pavement, and a broad ovall. [2]

Q. 13: where shall j find the key of your lodge? Yes [?=*Ans:*] Three foot and an half from the lodge door under a perpend esler and a green divot. But under the lap of my liver where all my secrets of my heart lie.

Q. 14: Which is the key of your lodge? *Ans:* aweel hung tongue.

Q. 15: where lies the key? *Ans:* In the bone box.

After the masons have examined you by all or some of these Questions and that you have answered them exactly and mad thesignes, they will acknowledge you, but not amaster mason or fellow croft, but only as as [?an] apprentice, soe they will say I see you have been in the kitchine, but I know not if you have been in the hall. *Ans:* I have been in the hall as weel as in the kitchine.

[1] *Perpend, parpen:* a stone which passes through a wall from side to side, having two smooth vertical faces (O.E.D.).

[2] *Broad ovall:* ?broached ornel. Broached: worked with a chisel (O.E.D.). Ornel, urnall, urnell: a kind of soft white building stone (O.E.D.). The terms "Parpeincoins," "pament," and "urnel" figure in the Rochester Castle Building Account, 1368 (*Arch. Cant.* ii, 114).

Q. 1 : Are you a fellow craft? *Ans:* Yes.
Q. 2 : How many points of the fellowship are ther? *Ans:* fyve, viz., foot to foot, Knee to Kn[ee], Heart to Heart, Hand to Hand, and ear to ear. *Then make the sign of fellowship and shake hand and you will be acknowledged a true mason. The words are in the* 1 *of the Kings Ch* 7, *v* 21, *and in* 2 *Chr: ch* 3 *verse last.*

The conclusion of the examination shows, first, that the fellowcraft or master mason (which were equivalent terms in Scotland at this period) had secrets distinct from those of an entered apprentice; and secondly, that only the fellowcraft was acquainted with what are called "the five points of the fellowship." Further reference will be made to these two matters shortly.

"The form of giving the mason word" is a series of instructions to those admitting "the person to take the word," and indicates in a general way what was to be said to him and what he was to say. After he had taken an oath of secrecy, in which he swore not to reveal by word or writing any part of what he should see or hear, nor to draw it with the point of a sword, or any other instrument, upon the snow or sand, he was to go out with the youngest mason from whom he was to learn "the signe and the postures and words of his entrie." He then rejoined the company and said the words of his entry, which read:[1]

Here come I, the youngest and last entered apprentice, As I am sworn by God and St Jhon, by the square and compass and common judge,[2] to attend my masters service at the honourable lodge, from munday in the

[1] To facilitate reading, the punctuation has been modernized, and such sentences as appear to be instructions have been printed in italics.

[2] In mining, a *judge* is a staff used to measure the depth of holes (O.E.D.). Jamieson's *Scottish Dictionary* defines *jedge* as a gauge or standard. Amongst masons, it possibly referred to the *virga geometricalis*, or measuring rod, with which the foundation or ground plan of a building was marked out. (See Note by Knoop and Jones on "Latlaying the Groundwork," *Misc. Lat.*, Sept. 1937). Pictures of mediaeval masons sometimes show them with a square, compasses and a measuring rod, as in Libergier's tomb slab in Rheims Cathedral (Coulton, *Art and the Reformation*, 140).

morning till saturday at night and to keep the keyes therof, under no less pain then haveing my tongue cut out under my chin, and of being buried within the flood mark, where no man shall know; *then he makes the sign, again with drawing his hand under his chin alongst his throat, which denotes that it be cut out in caise he break his word.*[1]

This shows that, whatever other objects the formal admission might have, it served to emphasize the duties which the entered apprentice owed to his master.

In at least one Scottish operative lodge in 1670, namely, the Lodge of Aberdeen, the entered apprentice, in addition to receiving the Mason Word at his entry, had read to him the "Mason Charter," which was the version of the Old Charges now described as the *Aberdeen MS.*, and also the Laws and Statutes of the Lodge.[2] As the reading of these two documents would require the best part of an hour, the proceedings at the admission of an entered apprentice, if the Aberdeen practice was at all general,[3] must have been considerably longer than a perusal of the *Edinburgh Register House MS.* would suggest.

TWO DISTINCT CEREMONIES IN 1696

Reverting to our MS., it may be noted that at the conclusion of what may be described as the ceremony, the word was circulated amongst those present and was finally

---

[1] These words of entry may be compared with those still used at an old practice of the Scoon and Perth Lodge No. 3, called the Baptism, which is performed at the time of refreshment. The Master, taking a little whiskey and water in his hand, pours it on the head of the newly made apprentice, who repeats after the Master these words: "Here comes I the youngest and last made mason willing to do my Master's bidding from Monday morning to Saturday night. . . ." There is a reference in the Lodge minutes of 22 January 1741, to washing the newly admitted apprentice's head, and the likelihood is that the practice goes back to operative days (Crawford Smith, *History of the Ancient Masonic Lodge of Scoon and Perth*, 101).

[2] See quotation from the Mark Book of the Lodge, in Miller, 21. The Charter and the Statutes of 1670 are printed in the Appendices to that book.

[3] In addition to the Lodge of Aberdeen, the Lodges of Aitchison's Haven, Kilwinning, Melrose, Stirling, and Dumfries all appear to have possessed versions of the Old Charges dating from the second half of the seventeenth century (Poole, *Old Charges*, 15–17).

given to the candidate by the Master. These signs and words were those of an entered apprentice, and, as the MS. points out, there were others belonging to a master mason or fellowcraft, which were imparted as follows. All entered apprentices were ordered out of the company and none suffered to stay but masters. Then, "he who is to be admitted a member of fellowship" knelt and took an oath of secrecy, after which he went out with the youngest master to learn "the posture and signes of fellowship." On returning, he made the master's sign and said the former words of entry, but leaving out the "common judge"; the masons then whispered the word among themselves, and finally the master gave him the word and the grip. There is nothing in the MS. as to the nature of the master's sign, word or grip, though some indications are given regarding the apprentice's secrets.

The fact that in 1696 there were two distinct ceremonies, if they may be so described, one applying to entered apprentices and one to fellowcrafts or masters, raises two questions: first, who the entered apprentices were, and secondly, whether both ceremonies were equally old.

ENTERED APPRENTICES AND THEIR SECRETS

The object of obtaining the Mason Word was presumably to acquire a method of recognition, and thereby to secure certain advantages in the matter of employment, and possibly of relief.[1] Ordinary apprentices were not free to seek work independently of the masters to whom they were bound,[2] and would therefore have no need of secret methods of recognition. Nor would they require

[1] Murray Lyon, 28, and Miller, 30. It may be noted that masons were not the only craftsmen to possess a "word." The squaremen, i.e., wrights, and possibly members of other building crafts, received the "squaremen word" (Murray Lyon, 23). O.E.D. defines squareman as "A carpenter, stone-cutter or other workman who regularly uses a square for adjusting or testing his work," and notes its earliest occurrence as 1790. Actually, one of the signatories of the so-called St. Clair charter of 1628 describes himself as "deakin of squarmen" (Murray Lyon, 68).

[2] In London in the seventeenth century apprentices sometimes worked apart from their masters, but probably only on jobs to which they had been sent by them (Knoop and Jones, *The London Mason in the Seventeenth Century*, 64, 65).

relief, since their masters maintained them. The apprentice who was given the Mason Word could not, therefore, have been an ordinary apprentice. The explanation probably lies in the fact, that in Scotland in the seventeenth century, and possibly earlier, apprentices and entered apprentices apparently formed two distinct classes or grades,[1] the entered apprentices hardly being apprentices at all in the ordinary sense of the word, but rather journeyman ex-apprentices. In Scotland, the Schaw Statutes of 1598 [2] provided that an apprentice must be bound for at least seven years, and that, except by special permission, a further period of seven years must elapse before he could be made a fellowcraft. During this second term of seven years,[3] or less, as the case might be, the ex-apprentice was apparently an entered apprentice, and normally worked as a journeyman for a master, though the Schaw Statutes did permit an entered apprentice to undertake a limited amount of work on his own account. That this general ordinance applied locally is shown by the Mutual Agreement of 1658, which regulated the affairs of the Lodge of Perth.[4] This provided that no entered apprentice should leave his master or masters to take any work or task work above 40s. Scots. Further, it was expressly provided that he was not to take an apprentice. At Kilwinning in 1659, two fellowcrafts and one entered apprentice out of each quarter, together with the Deacon and Warden, were appointed to

[1] A Minute of the Aitchison's Haven Lodge, dated 27 December 1655 (*A.Q.C.*, xxiv, 41), records that apprentices were not to be made entered apprentices under the sum of twelve pounds Scots.

[2] Printed in Murray Lyon, 9, and Knoop and Jones, *The Mediaeval Mason*, 258.

[3] Cases of masons serving double apprenticeships occurred in England in the seventeenth century. Thus Richard Varney of Islip, stonemason, examined in the Chancellor's Court at Oxford, 26 April 1681, stated that "he served his father (though he was his eldest son) more than a double apprenticeship"; John Saunders of Denton, stonemason, stated, on the same occasion, that he had served his father a double apprenticeship. [Abstract (very kindly lent to G. P. Jones and myself by the Rev. H. E. Salter) of papers labelled "1681 M" in the Oxford University Archives.] These double apprenticeships, however, were hardly analogous to the Scottish practice of apprenticeship and entered apprenticeship.

[4] Crawford Smith, chap. v.

meet each year at Ayr to deal with transgressors.[1] At
Melrose, the entered apprentices were parties to the
Mutual Agreement of 1675, which regulated the affairs
of the Lodge.[2] At Aberdeen in 1670, the Laws and
Statutes of the Lodge show that entered apprentices received the benefit of the Mason Word at their entry,[3] and
that they became eligible for the fellowship three years
later; further, the Mark Book of the Lodge shows that
each entered apprentice had his mark,[4] and the same was
the case at Dumfries in 1687.[5] The Schaw Statutes of
1598 provided that no master or fellowcraft should be
received, except in the presence of six masters and two
entered apprentices, and the early Minutes of the Lodge of
Edinburgh prove that this requirement was observed.[6]

This evidence shows clearly that entered apprentices in
Scotland had a real, if subordinate, share in the government
of the craft and in its privileges. Their position can be
compared with that occupied by the Yeomanry in the
London Masons' Company. It is inconceivable that either
in London or in Scotland, the ordinary apprentice had any
say in the management of the craft, or that he enjoyed any
privileges; his was purely a position of servitude until the
period for which he was bound had expired. Thereupon,
in London he might be made a freeman and become part
of the Yeomanry of the Masons' Company;[7] in Scotland

[1] Minute of the Lodge, dated 20 December 1659, quoted in R. Wylie,
History of the Mother Lodge, Kilwinning, 2nd ed., 60.

[2] Printed in W. F. Vernon, *History of Freemasonry in Roxburghshire ana
Selkirkshire*, 13.

[3] There is nothing in the *Edinburgh Register House MS.* to indicate when
the entered apprentice received the benefit of the Mason Word. It merely
refers to "the person to take the word."

[4] See page from Mark Book reproduced in Miller, facing p. 28.

[5] Regulation of the Lodge of Dumfries, approved 2 June 1687, printed
in J. Smith, *History of the Old Lodge of Dumfries*, 9. The use of marks
on work to enable the craftsman to be identified was not peculiar to masons.
In London the Helmet-makers, Blacksmiths, Bladesmiths and Brasiers used
them (Riley, *Memorials of London*, 238, 361, 569, 626.)

[6] Murray Lyon, 79.

[7] Actually rather fewer than 50 per cent. of the apprentices bound in
London took up their freedom (*The London Mason in the Seventeenth Century*,
63).

he became an entered apprentice and received the benefit of the Mason Word. In due course, a yeoman in London might be accepted into the Livery, and an entered apprentice in Scotland might be received as a master or fellow-craft.[1] There was, however, an important difference: the former promotion was the exception rather than the rule;[2] the latter promotion, so far as one can tell, was the rule rather than the exception.[3] A rather better analogy is provided by the London carpenters who, under an Ordinance of 1607,[4] were forbidden to have an apprentice until they had been "free" three years and had served at least one year with a freeman of the Company.

So far as I am aware, the term "entered apprentice" occurs in operative masonry only in Scotland. It is commonly held that the entered apprentice was so called "because entered in the Lodge books,"[5] but this cannot be regarded as a complete explanation. The Schaw Statutes of 1598 distinguished between (i) "receiving" an apprentice and (ii) "entering" an apprentice: "receiving" apparently took

---

[1] In London there was no prescribed minimum period, and very occasionally an apprentice was made a freeman, and accepted into the Livery, on the same day, e.g. Edward Strong, jun., in 1698 (*The London Mason in the Seventeenth Century*, 45 n). In Scotland, although the Schaw Statutes contemplated an entered apprenticeship of seven years, except by special permission, the period at Aberdeen in 1670 was three years. At Glasgow, in the early seventeenth century, the usual period appears to have been two years, to judge by the following:

It would appear from the Minutes [of the Incorporation of Masons], 9 February 1613, and 5 February 1617, that nine years was the customary endurance of an Apprenticeship, viz., seven years to learn the trade, and two for meat and fee (Cruikshank, *Sketch of the Incorporation of Masons and the Lodge of Glasgow St. John*, 63).

[2] The Quarterage Book of the Masons' Company shows that in 1663 there were 45 members of the Livery, including assistants, as compared with 143 members of the Yeomanry; in 1677 the corresponding figures were 71 and 162 (*The London Mason in the Seventeenth Century*, 8, 9).

[3] That there were exceptions is shown by the fact that, in Edinburgh in the seventeenth century, it was not unusual for entered apprentices on the expiry of their entered apprenticeship to seek employment as journeymen, without having been admitted as fellowcrafts (Murray Lyon, 28).

[4] Jupp and Pocock, *Historical Account of the Worshipful Company of Carpenters*, 423.

[5] Kenning's *Cyclopaedia of Freemasonry*, 201.

place at the outset of his career, and "entering" at some later, but unspecified, date, presumably at the expiration of seven years' servitude. The Statutes further provided that the name of the apprentice and the date of his "receiving" should be booked, and that, in due course, the date of his "entering" should be booked. Thus "entering" could hardly have meant simply that his name was entered in a book, as that had also been done when he was "received." It related, more probably, to his admission or entry into the ranks of the time-expired or fully qualified apprentices. The term "entered apprentice" occurs in the forms "enterprentice" [1] and "interprintice". [2] *Enter* and *inter* are both Scottish forms of *entire*, so that the term may have denoted *entire apprentice*, i.e., complete or fully qualified apprentice.

Three pieces of evidence may be cited in support of this opinion. First, a Minute of the Aitchison's Haven Lodge, dated 2 January 1600, records that Andrew Patten was "enterit prenteis to Johne Crafurd his maister". [3] As a Minute of 7 June 1599 records that Andrew Patten had served six years of his apprenticeship at that date, [4] it follows that he had served about seven years when he was "entered". Secondly, a Minute of the Lodge of Edinburgh, dated 3 February 1601, records that Andrew Hamilton apprentice to John Watt, was "enterit . . . as past prenteis to ye said Johnne Wat his m[aiste]r." [5] This clearly shows that Andrew Hamilton had served his time before being "entered." Thirdly, Article XIV of the *Regius MS.* requires

> . . . if that the master a prentice have,
> *Entirely* then that he him teach.

If originally an apprentice was *entered* as an *entire* apprentice, confusion between *entered* and *entire* might easily have led to *entire* apprentice being changed to *entered* apprentice.

The secrets communicated to entered apprentices were

---

[1] *Trinity College, Dublin MS.*   [2] *Sloane MS.* 3329.
[3] *A.Q.C.*, xxiv, 36.   [4] *Ibid.*, 35.   [5] Murray Lyon, 79.

probably not the essential ones, but means of recognition, safeguarded with less caution than the principal secrets, and regarded partly as a joke. The possession of such secrets doubtless carried with it fewer privileges. The first two conclusions are suggested by a study of the *Edinburgh Register House MS.* (i) This shows that a good deal of horseplay was associated with the imparting of the entered apprentice secrets. Thus the oath was to be administered only "after a great many ceremonies to frighten" the candidate; when outside with the youngest mason, the candidate was to be frightened "with 1000 ridiculous postures and grimaces" before being given the sign, postures, and words of entry; after rejoining the company he was to "make a ridiculous bow" and "put off his hat after a very foolish manner." This horseplay may be compared with the practices common at the admission of freshmen to universities in mediaeval and later times,[1] or with the tests imposed upon newcomers to the Hanseatic factory at Bergen.[2] That something of this horseplay was liable to be introduced into the early speculative Lodges, is clearly implied by one of the by-laws of the Lodge constituted at the Maid's Head, Norwich, in May 1724, which reads: "6. That no ridiculous trick be played with any person when he is admitted."[3] These by-laws are stated to have been "recommended by our Worthy Bᵣₒ Dʳ Desaguliers" [Grand Master in 1719 and Deputy Grand Master in 1722–23 and 1725], and may be regarded as reflecting the desire of the recently formed Grand Lodge to suppress such horseplay. On the other hand, no corresponding fooling is mentioned in the *Edinburgh Register House MS.* in connection with being "admitted a member of fellowship." (ii) It is very noticeable, as previously mentioned, that whereas the MS. gives various indications as to the nature of the entered apprentice's secrets, it preserves a complete silence regarding those of the fellowcraft or master.

[1] R. S. Rait, *Life in the Mediaeval University*, chap. vi.
[2] Helen Zimmern, *The Hansa Towns*, 144–47.
[3] G. W. Daynes, *A.Q.C.*, xxxvii, 38.

RELATIVE AGE OF THE TWO CEREMONIES

Regarding the second question, the considerations I have just mentioned suggest the conclusion that the giving of the Mason Word originally concerned fellowcrafts only, and that the participation in it of entered apprentices was a later development. When that development took place is uncertain; very possibly it occurred when the category of entered apprentices, intermediate between apprentices and fellowcrafts, was first established, probably at some date prior to 1598. This doubtless represented an attempt to limit the number of potential masters, which rather suggests that it originated in the sixteenth century, a period when many gilds tended to develop restrictive policies. The Minutes of Aitchison's Haven Lodge [1] show that as early as 1598, when a new entered apprentice was admitted, he chose two entered apprentices as his intenders and instructors, and when a new fellowcraft was admitted, he chose two fellowcrafts as his intenders and instructors. If these intenders corresponded to the "youngest mason" and the "youngest master" of the *Edinburgh Register House MS.*, who taught the candidates the signs and postures, then it may well be that there were two sets of secrets in 1598, and that it was these which the intenders imparted to the newly admitted entered apprentices and fellowcrafts respectively. On the other hand, it must be noted that, whereas the Schaw Statutes of 1598 required the name and mark of every fellowcraft or master to be booked (there being no corresponding stipulation concerning the entered apprentice, who presumably had no mark), at Aberdeen in 1670 the names and marks of entered apprentices, as well as those of fellowcrafts, were recorded in the Mark Book. This suggests that the entered apprentice of 1670 enjoyed more privileges than his predecessor of 1598, but does not preclude the latter from having enjoyed some privileges.

If the giving of the Mason Word originally concerned fellowcrafts only, as I am inclined to think, the question

[1] R. E. Wallace-James, "The Minute Book of the Aitchison's Haven Lodge, 1598–1764," *A.Q.C.*, xxiv.

at once arises whether the secrets and ceremony appertaining to apprentices were new, or whether they were those previously given to fellowcrafts. The words of entry, being common to apprentices and fellowcrafts, apart from the omission of a reference to the "common judge," were almost certainly old, and the same is probably true of the test questions and answers. I think it not unlikely that any signs and words were also old, and that it was the fellowcrafts who had been provided with new and more elaborate methods of recognition. To explain why I incline to this view, it is necessary to examine more closely what is known about the Mason Word in relation to fellowcrafts.

THE FIVE POINTS OF FELLOWSHIP

As previously mentioned, the *Edinburgh Register House MS.* tells little about the giving of the Mason Word to fellowcrafts, but the last question and answer clearly show that the person to be "admitted a member of fellowship" was made acquainted with what are called "the five points of the fellowship, viz., foot to foot, knee to knee, heart to heart, hand to hand and ear to ear." Further light, however, is thrown on the subject by the recently discovered *Graham MS.*,[1] which bears the date 1726.

THE *GRAHAM MS.* AND THE NOAH STORY

The *Graham MS.* appears to be the same type of document as the *Edinburgh Register House MS.*, namely, a mason's *aide mémoire*, although it bears quite a different heading, viz., "The whole Institutions of free Masonry opened and proved by the best of tradition and still some referance to scripture." It consists of two parts, the first an examination, along somewhat similar lines to the *Edinburgh MS.*, the second an exposition, in the form of a "lecture," of legendary matter, chiefly concerning Noah, Bezaleel and King Solomon, which bears little resemblance to the events recorded in the historical section of the MS. *Constitutions of Masonry.*

---

[1] This is named after the writer, Thomas Graham, and belongs to the Rev. H. I. Robinson, Londesborough Rectory, York, who first drew attention to it when he was initiated in 1936. A photographic reproduction, with introduction by Bro. Poole, appears in *A.Q.C.*, vol. 1 (1937).

Before referring more fully to the legendary matter, I should state that the *Graham MS.* concludes with a cryptic reference to masons' secrets, and an enumeration of what are called "five points of free Masons fellowshipe which is foot to foot, knee to knee, breast to breast, cheeck to cheeck and hand to Back." The reference to freemasons' secrets reads thus:

> So all [i.e. King Solomon's Temple] Being ffinised then was the secrets off ffree Masonry ordered a right as is now and will be to the E End of the world for such as do rightly understand it—in 3 parts in refferance to the blesed trinity who made all things yet in 13 brenches in refferances to Christ and his 12 apostles which is as ffollows aword ffor adeveine[1] Six ffor for the clargey and 6 ffor the ffellow craft.

The "three parts" conceivably refer to the three Degrees, which, as I shall attempt to show later, probably existed by 1726. I have no suggestions to offer regarding the "13 branches," which, near the end of the MS., are set out thus:

Your first is

your second is   your third is

....

your twelfth is   your thirteenth is

More important for our present purpose is the enumeration of the "five points of free Masons fellowshipe," as the occurrence of the same five points in the legendary matter relating to Noah doubtless provides one possible explanation of their origin. The rather gruesome story is briefly as follows: Noah's three sons, desirous of finding something about him to lead them to the valuable secret which their father had possessed—for all things needful for the new world were in the Ark with Noah—went to Noah's grave, agreeing beforehand that if they did not find the very thing itself, the first thing they found was to be to them as a secret. They found nothing in the grave except the dead body; when the finger was gripped it came away, and so with the wrist and the elbow. They then reared up the dead body,

----

[1] *Adeveine:* ? a Divine Being.

supporting it by setting foot to foot, knee to knee, breast to breast, cheek to cheek and hand to back. Thereupon "one said here is yet marow in this bone and the second said but a dry bone and the third said it stinketh.[1] So they agreed for to give it a name as is known to free masonry to this day."

The bone, being the first thing found, must presumably have some significance. Whether the phrase "marrow in this bone" is significant, is not so certain. It may be noted that the word *marrow*, in addition to its ordinary meaning, had certainly another, and possibly a symbolical meaning, for Scottish masons. It was used in Northern Middle English, and in Scotland down to the nineteenth century, to denote "partner," "fellow," "mate," and it is not uncommon in that sense in sixteenth- and seventeenth-century Scottish building accounts.[2] "Here is yet marrow in this bone" may thus have been a reminder that fellowship was of the essence of masonry. It is also possible that "marrow in this bone" may have been intended to serve as a mnemonic.

PRICHARD'S *MASONRY DISSECTED* AND THE HIRAM STORY

Another possible explanation of the five points of fellowship is provided by a story relating to Hiram, of which the oldest-known form is that in Prichard's *Masonry Dissected*, first published in 1730.[3] According to this version of the story, three masons murdered Hiram, King Solomon's master of the works at the building of the Temple, in an attempt to extort from him the secrets of a master mason. On his being missed, fifteen fellowcrafts were ordered to search for him, and they agreed, that if they did not find the word in or about him, the first word should be the master's

---

[1] *It stinketh:* possibly a descendant of mediaeval and sixteenth-century satires on relics. Cf. *The Four PP*, ptd. ? 1545, of John Heywood (1497–1580), in which the Pardoner offers the Apothecary the "blessed jaw-bone" of All Hallows, and bids him kiss it devoutly. The Apothecary does so, and recoils with disgust—

... me-thinketh
That All Hallows' breath stinketh.

[2] E.g. "Item to Thom Crauford and his m[ar]rowis for 343 feet ashlar ... £5 17*s*. 10*d*." Edinburgh Register House, Master of Works Accounts, vol. 4, fo. 7, Holyrood House, 1535–36.

[3] Masonic Reprints XII, Lodge of Research, Leicester, 1929.

word. Ultimately his body was found under a covering of green moss,[1] and King Solomon ordered that it should be taken up and decently buried. When they took him by the forefinger the skin came off, whereupon they took a firmer grip of his hand and raised him by the five points of fellowship, viz., hand to hand, foot to foot, cheek to cheek, knee to knee and hand to back.

THE POSSIBLE ORIGIN OF THE NOAH AND HIRAM STORIES

The marked similarities between the Noah story and the Hiram story, in its oldest-known form, are very striking; both have the same main *motif*—the attempt to obtain a secret from a dead body, and both have the same subsidiary *motif*—the intention to provide a substituted secret, failing the discovery of a genuine one. Where either story originally came from, or how it became associated with masonry, is unknown. It is, however, possible that the Noah story had some connection with the narrative, in Genesis ix. 21–27, of the shaming of Noah, to which it is in some respects parallel. In Genesis, Noah was asleep; in the *Graham MS.* story, he was dead; but the exposure of his person in the former story, and the exhumation of his body in the latter, both offended against the respect due to a progenitor. In Genesis, Ham was the chief offender, on which account his progeny was cursed, and he is perhaps also to be regarded as the ringleader in the original of the *Graham MS.* story.

The stories of Noah and Hiram call to mind the fact that in Biblical instances of the miraculous restoration of life, the prophet or apostle lay full length upon the body and breathed into its face. Three cases are cited in the Bible—namely, those of Elijah, who raised the widow's son from the dead (1 Kings xvii. 17–23); of Elisha, who raised the son of the Shunammite woman (2 Kings iv. 34–35); and of St. Paul, who raised a young man named Eutychus (Acts xx. 9–12). In the second case the process is described in detail:

---

[1] The statement that the body was found "under a covering of green moss" may be compared with the statement in the *Edinburgh Register House MS.* (see p. 83 above) that the key of the Lodge is hidden "under a perpend esler and a green divot."

34. And he [Elisha] went up, and lay upon the child, and put his mouth upon his mouth, and his eyes upon his eyes, and his hands upon his hands: and he stretched himself upon the child; and the flesh of the child waxed warm.

35. Then he returned, and walked in the house to and fro; and went up, and stretched himself upon him: and the child sneezed seven times, and the child opened his eyes.

Here complete coincidence between living and dead was established twice, first by placing mouth to mouth, eyes to eyes and hands to hands, and secondly, by stretching at full length upon the body. It is thus not impossible that the original stories of Noah and Hiram may have been those of attempts to restore these men to life, because their secrets had died with them.

The Biblical examples show that the idea of complete coincidence of living and dead was to restore the dead to life. This would develop into necromantic practices, and in the sixteenth and seventeenth centuries the idea would survive only as necromancy.[1] It would seem not inconceivable that one story was modelled on the other, and that the original story rested on an old tradition connecting Ham, son of Noah, with magic and the black arts. The disinterment of Noah was clearly an act of necromancy, and it is therefore pertinent to note that Ham, son of Noah, is connected in mediaeval tradition, if not with necromancy in its narrower sense, at any rate with the black arts.[2] The tradition associating Ham with necromancy survived as late as the sixteenth century, when it is found in an English work, Reginald Scot's *Discoverie of Witchcraft* (1586).[3] It may further be noted that the five points of fellowship, suggesting as they do that two bodies were made to coincide, presum-

[1] Necromancy: the pretended art of revealing future events, etc., by means of communication with the dead (O.E.D.).

[2] Cf. Vincent de Beauvais, *Speculum Historiale*, book ii, chap. ci.

[3] In this book (ed. Montague Summers, p. 222) it is said of the devil Gaap, or Tap, that "certaine necromancers . . . offered sacrifices and burnt-offerings unto him and to call him up they exercised an art saieng that *Salomon* the wise made it, which is false; for it was rather *Cham*, the sonne of *Noah* who after the floud began first to invocate wicked spirits."

97

ably with object of the knowledge possessed by one passing to the other, also savour of popular superstition, and they support the possibility that the origin of the story must be sought in witchcraft or folklore. The fact that the Mason Word was linked by at least two seventeenth-century Scottish writers, Henry Adamson and Robert Kirk, with the subject of second sight,[1] conceivably points to the same conclusion.

THE *SLOANE MS.* 3329

Yet one other manuscript relating to the Mason Word, namely, *Sloane MS.* 3329,[2] calls for attention. This tract is headed "A Narrative of the Freemasons word and signes," and differs in character from the *Edinburgh Register House MS.* and the *Graham MS.*, as it does not appear to be a mason's *aide mémoire*, but a collection of notes on the Mason Word, apparently gathered by the writer from various sources. It contains (i) an account of a dozen signs by which an operative mason could make himself known to a fellow mason; (ii) a description of a fellowcraft's grip and of a master's grip, the latter in two forms; (iii) two series of questions and answers, resembling those of the *Edinburgh Register House* and *Graham MSS.*; (iv) a brief reference to the master's word—*mahabyn*—and the method of communicating it; (v) an oath. *Mahabyn* is very similar to the form *matchpin*, which is given as the master's word in the *Trinity College, Dublin MS.*

[1] Thus (i) Henry Adamson (*The Muses' Threnodie*, Edinburgh, 1638) says: "We have the mason word and second sight." (ii) When Rev. R. Kirk dined in October 1689, with Dr. Stillingfleet, Bishop-elect of Worcester, the conversation turned on second sight. In the midst of the record of that conversation occurs the sentence: "The Dr. called the Mason word a Rabbinical mystery, where I discovered somewhat of it" [R. Kirk, *London in 1689-90*, printed in *Trans. Lond. and Mid. Arch. Soc.* N.S. VII (1933), 139]. (iii) R. Kirk in *The Secret Commonwealth* (1933 ed., 107-8) enumerates five curiosities in Scotland "not much observed to be elsewhere": (*a*) The Brounies, (*b*) The Mason Word, (*c*) Second Sight, (*d*) Charmes, (*e*) A being Proof of Lead, Iron and Silver. Whether this association is a mere coincidence, or whether it implies some kind of connection and, if so, what, there is no evidence to show.

[2] This British Museum MS. consists of a double sheet, written on three and a half sides, bound up in a large volume, on the fly-leaf of which Sir Hans Sloane has written: "Loose papers of mine concerning curiosities."

The fact that the signs and words are associated in the *Sloane MS.* with operative *freemasons*, strongly suggests an immediate English source for the document, the word "freemason" being unknown in Scotland as a trade designation; the reference to "interprintices" [entered apprentices] and fellowcrafts, on the other hand, points to an ultimate Scottish origin, as these terms were used only in Scotland in operative masonry; the word "attenders" [intenders], which occurs in the oath, also suggests Scottish origin, as the practice of appointing intenders to be responsible for teaching entered apprentices [1] did not extend to England, so far as I am aware. The use of the expression "this is bose or hollow" also suggests a Scottish origin.[2] Dr. Schofield, of the British Museum Manuscripts Department, who recently examined the manuscript, gives the date as *circa* 1700. As we know from the *Edinburgh Register House MS.* that a master's word and sign existed at least as early as 1696, there is nothing in the document which makes this date improbable,[3] though the distinction drawn between the terms "fellowcraft" and "master" is not found in Scotland at such an early date. The five points of fellowship, as such, are not mentioned in

---

[1] *Intender, intendar:* occurs in this sense in the Laws and Statutes of the Lodge of Aberdeen, 1670, and in the Schaw Statutes, 1598, as well as in the Minutes of the Aitchison's Haven Lodge. Craigie, *Dict. Older Scottish Tongue,* defines *Attender, Attendar,* "One who attends on another, or to some duty."

[2] See Wright, *English Dialect Dictionary,* under *boss;* also Craigie, *op. cit.,* which gives *bos, boys, bose, bois, adj.,* hollow, concave, perhaps from *bos, boce,* etc., a leather bottle for liquids.

[3] The late Brother J. Walter Hobbs stated some years ago that the earliest instance he had been able to trace of certain words which occur in the oath, namely "without any manner of equivocation or mentall reservation," was in the Sovereign's Accession Oath as revised by Parliament for use on the accession of James II in 1685 (*A.Q.C.,* xxxvii, 36), which suggests, if it does no more, that the *Sloane MS.* is not earlier than 1685. On the other hand, Brother Poole (*ibid.,* 8) refers to the suggestion made by Findel [*History of Freemasonry* (1869), 118 n.], which he regards as not altogether impossible, that the *Sloane MS.* was among the papers Plot had before him when compiling his *History of Staffordshire* (1686). The grounds for making the suggestion are: (i) that no earlier document is known especially mentioning that a Brother must come down, even "from the top of a steeple", in answer to a sign, and (ii) that in at least one place the Plot account agrees practically verbatim with the *Sloane MS.*

the *Sloane MS.*, but the method of communicating the master's word, as described there, embodies four of the points.

THE MASON WORD

Both the Noah and the Hiram stories show that those engaged in the search did not find "the very thing itself," or "the word," for which they were looking, and that they had consequently to content themselves with substitutes. This suggests the possibility that there was a genuine secret somewhere in the background, which might conceivably be THE Mason Word, to which no kind of direct reference appears to be made in any of the MSS. It is doubtless very tempting, on the strength of such hints as can be gathered from the limited material available, and by reading between the lines, to conjecture what THE Mason Word was, and who shared a knowledge of it, always assuming that there was such a word. As the MS. *Constitutions of Masonry* and the manuscripts which we have more particularly in mind this evening, all refer, directly or indirectly, to Jewish history, there would appear to be a presumption that THE Mason Word was connected in some way with the Scriptures, and it is conceivable, in view of the complete silence on the subject of the MSS., that it was the Name of God, which according to Jewish tradition was never to be pronounced. If this was so, THE Mason Word was very possibly communicated amongst masons solely by means of a sign. In support of this very tentative surmise, it may be pointed out that the idea of a dread Demogorgon who was not to be named, occurs in sixteenth- and seventeenth-century literature both in Scotland and England, as can be illustrated from the writings of Sir David Lindsay (1490–1555),[1] Spenser (1552–99),[2] Milton (1608–74)[3] and Dryden (1631–1700).[4]

[1] Sir David Lindsay, *Works*, ed. D. Hamer, I. 266 [*Monarche* l. 2253], and III, 331, where the matter is fully discussed.
[2] Spenser, *Faerie Queene*, I. xxxvii, 7–9, refers to Gorgon as the deity whose name may not be used.
[3] Milton, *Paradise Lost*, II, 959.
[4] Dryden's rendering of *The Flower and the Leaf*, in *Poems*, Oxford ed., p. 333.

THE MASON WORD

Fascinating though such speculations may be, I only mention the possibility of THE Mason Word to show that it has not been overlooked. My object in this lecture is the much more prosaic task of attempting to give an account of the Mason Word as an operative institution, and to use such matter-of-fact evidence as is available, to construct a picture of the institution and the conditions governing its operation.

In this connection it must be borne in mind that the Mason Word was something of great practical importance to Scottish operative masons; so much so, that early in the eighteenth century one Lodge actually went to law to secure the right to give the Mason Word.[1] It was part of the machinery for preventing unqualified masons from working in the burghs, and corresponded to the steps taken by the London Masons' Company to preserve their monopoly of trade in the City.[2] There was, however, this important difference: the London regulations aimed at restraining, if not entirely preventing, "foreign" masons, i.e. masons who were not freemen of the city, from carrying on their trade in London, whereas the object of the Mason Word was to check so-called "cowans"[3] from doing the work of qualified masons. I know of no evidence to show that the Mason Word was in use amongst English operative masons, and think it quite possible that it was through the non-operative members of Scottish Lodges that English "accepted" or "adopted" masons first became acquainted with the subject.

AGE OF THE MASON WORD

Although it is almost certain that the area to which the Mason Word applied was Scotland, its age as an institution is more problematical: there is mention of it in seventeenth-century minute books of certain Scottish operative lodges[4]; the earliest-known printed reference to it occurs in Henry

[1] The Lodge of Journeymen Masons, Edinburgh (Murray Lyon, ch. xvi, and Seggie and Turnbull, *Annals of the Lodge of Journeymen Masons, No. 8*, ch. i).
[2] *The London Mason in the Seventeenth Century*, 10.
[3] *Cowan:* One who builds dry stone walls—applied derogatorily to one who does the work of a mason, but has not been regularly apprenticed or bred to the trade.... In 1707 Mother Kilwinning Lodge defined the Cowan as a Mason "without the word" (O.E.D.).
[4] Murray Lyon, 22.

Adamson's *The Muses' Threnodie*, a metrical account of Perth and its neighbourhood, published in Edinburgh in 1638 [1]: "We have the Mason word and second sight." This clearly implies that the Mason Word was a well-established institution in Scotland by 1638. If, as appears likely, it was a privilege associated with the termination of an apprenticeship, or the admission to a fellowship, it might be as old as the system of apprenticeship. In London, that system dates from the early thirteenth century, and outside London from the late thirteenth century, but no reference to a mason's apprentice in England and Wales has been traced before the end of the fourteenth century.[2] How early the apprenticeship of masons developed in Scotland, I am unable to say, but as the Seal of Cause of 1475, which regulated the trades of the Masons and Wrights in Edinburgh,[3] provided for a seven years' apprenticeship, it is possible that the Mason Word as an institution in Scotland goes back to the fifteenth century. In England the earliest-known printed reference occurs in 1672 in Andrew Marvell's *Rehearsal Transprosed*, part i: "As those that have the Mason's word secretly discern one another."[4]

I am disposed to think that the scope of the Mason Word gradually grew; I have already suggested that the imparting of secret methods of recognition to entered apprentices was probably a new development at some date prior to 1598; I am also inclined to think that an elaboration of the secrets imparted to fellowcrafts took place during the seventeenth century. In Scotland in 1696, to judge by the *Edinburgh Register House MS.*, before a candidate could be admitted to the fellowship, all apprentices had to retire, doubtless because the candidate, after being instructed outside by the youngest master, had to re-enter the company, make the master's sign, and advance and put himself into the "posture" to receive the word, which was given him by the

[1] Henry Adamson, a Master of Arts and well-known citizen of Perth, was very possibly a non-operative member of the Lodge of Scoon and Perth, No. 3 (Crawford Smith, 41, 42).

[2] *The Mediaeval Mason*, 160, 161.

[3] Murray Lyon, 248.

[4] Grosart's edition of Marvell's Works, vol. iii, p. 55, quoted in *Misc. Lat.*, N.S., xvii, 134.

Master, together with the grip. In 1598, the Schaw Statutes, which were to be observed by all master masons in Scotland, provided that two entered apprentices, in addition to six masters or fellows, should be present at the admission of a fellow, which implies that the admission at the end of the sixteenth century must have been different from what it was at the end of the seventeenth, as the master's sign could not be made, nor the posture assumed, in the presence of two entered apprentices, though a word might have been communicated in a whisper. The presumption, therefore, is that there was no "posture" in 1598, and if, as seems likely, the "posture" implied the "five points of fellowship," then it follows that the "five points," together with the story explaining them, were probably not associated with the Mason Word in 1598.

The practices connected with the communication of the Mason Word probably changed quite as much during the seventeenth century, as did masonic ceremonies during the eighteenth, a matter to which I shall refer shortly. As a possible explanation of seventeenth-century development, I would tentatively suggest that the five points of fellowship may have been introduced from witchcraft or folklore, without any explanation being given in the first instance, Scottish working men at that period being not unacquainted with such practices. In the second half of the century, to judge by the dates of most of the surviving Scottish versions of the MS. *Constitutions of Masonry*,[1] the Scottish lodges adopted the Old Charges and caused them to be read to the entered apprentices at their admission.[2] It is not inconceivable, that in order to provide the fellowcrafts with some kind of corresponding history, and perhaps to supply an explanation of the "five points" for the benefit of the increasing number of non-operative masons,[3] a story was elaborated. This was possibly done, in part at least, by the utilization of existing traditions. The Noah story, with its distinctly necromantic flavour, would doubtless be formulated first; the Hiram story, further removed from witchcraft, but, in its oldest-

---

[1] See p. 85, note 3 above.   [2] Miller, 21.
[3] E.g. at Aberdeen in 1670 the non-operatives largely outnumbered the operatives (*ibid.*, 23).

known form, very similar in its *motifs* to the Noah story, would follow later. In each case, a very minor character in the legendary history of the MS. *Constitutions of Masonry* was made the principal figure of the story.

That the secrets and "five points of fellowship," communicated to fellowcrafts or masters, were a relatively late development, is also suggested by the fact that the so-called Master's Part (the prototype of the present Third Degree ceremony) was worked but little, if at all, in England at the time of the formation of Grand Lodge in 1717, or for some years afterwards.[1] It is, therefore, possible that just as a knowledge of the MS. *Constitutions of Masonry* was probably introduced from England into Scotland during the earlier part of the seventeenth century,[2] after the union of the two Crowns, or possibly during the reign of Elizabeth, so a knowledge of the Mason Word may have been introduced from Scotland into England about the same period, before the elaboration of the ceremony associated with the giving of the Mason Word had taken place. Thus many masons in England in the later seventeenth and early eighteenth centuries might be acquainted only with the older secrets and practices which in Scotland by that date had come to be associated with the giving of the Mason Word to entered apprentices, and might be ignorant of the newer and more carefully guarded and elaborate secrets restricted to fellowcrafts or masters.

On the other hand, if we are right in assuming that *Sloane MS.* 3329 was in the first instance derived from English sources, the master's word was known to some masons in England as early as *circa* 1700. It may be noted, also, that although the *Sloane MS.*, like the *Edinburgh Register House MS.*, recognizes a twofold series of secrets, the *Sloane MS.* associates them with (i) fellowcrafts and (ii) masters, whereas the *Edinburgh MS.* associates them with (i) entered apprentices and (ii) fellowcrafts or masters. As already indicated, there are grounds for thinking that originally the Mason Word was communicated only to

[1] Hughan, *Origin of the English Rite* (1925), 38 *folg.*
[2] Vibert, "The Early Freemasonry of England and Scotland," *A.Q.C.*, xliii, 208.

fellowcrafts, and it may be that whilst in Scotland the old secrets came ultimately to be communicated to entered apprentices and new secrets to fellowcrafts or masters, in England the old secrets were retained for communication to fellows, and new ones were given to masters.

TWOFOLD ORIGIN OF MASONIC CEREMONIES

Nothing shows more clearly the twofold origin of masonic ceremonies than the oath set out in *Sloane MS.* 3329, by which the candidate swore to keep secret "the mason word and everything therein contained" and truly to observe "the Charges in the Constitution." This confirms the Aberdeen practice, to which reference has already been made, that on the occasion when the Mason Word was communicated to an entered apprentice, a version of the MS. *Constitutions of Masonry* was read to him. At the end of another version of the MS. *Constitutions of Masonry*, known as the *Harris No.* 1 *MS.*, which dates from the second half of the seventeenth century, there is a note referring to the secrets which must never be committed to writing, and the manner of communicating them.[1] There is no evidence to show whether in the seventeenth century this MS. was used by operative masons or by "accepted" or "adopted" masons; but I am inclined to think it was the latter. That "accepted" or "adopted" masons in the later part of the seventeenth century did have secret signs and words, is borne out by the contemporary statement of John Aubrey, the antiquary, who wrote in the second half of the century, that members of the Fraternity of adopted masons were known to one another by certain signs and watchwords, and that the manner of their adoption was very formal and with an oath of secrecy.[2] It is confirmed

---

[1] The *Harris No.* 1 *MS.* is printed in *The Freemasons' Chronicle*, 30 December 1922. The note is printed in Poole's *Old Charges*, p. 23, as follows:

Then let the prson wch is to be made a Mason chuse out of the Lodge any one Mason who is to Instruct him in those Secrets wch must never be committed to Writeing which Mason he must alway Call his Tutor then let the Tutor take him into another Room and shew him all the whole Mistery that at his return he may Exercise with the rest of his fellow Masons.

[2] John Aubrey (1624–97), *Natural History of Wiltshire*, first printed in 1847.

also by a rough memorandum [1] referring to the several signs
and words of a freemason, written by Randle Holme III
on a scrap of paper, now bound up with B.M. *Harleian MS.*
2054, close to the version of the MS. *Constitutions of Masonry*
copied by him, with which it is thought to be connected,[2]
both documents probably being associated with a Lodge of
Freemasons held at Chester about the middle of the seventeenth century. That such signs and words were derived
from the Mason Word of the operatives, is strongly
suggested by the fact that when Dr. Desaguliers, the
prominent speculative mason, desired to visit the purely
operative Lodge of Edinburgh in 1721, he was found
"duly qualified in all points of masonry" and received as a
brother.[3]

THE *TRINITY COLLEGE, DUBLIN MS.*

On the subject of the connection between operative and
speculative masonry, I wish finally to draw attention to the
Trinity College, Dublin MS.[4] This bears the date 1711 in
an endorsement,[5] and resembles the *Edinburgh Register
House, Graham,* and *Sloane MSS.* in that it consists of a series
of test questions and answers, together with a memorandum
about signs and words. Like the *Edinburgh Register House
MS.*, it appears to be a mason's *aide mémoire*; on the other
hand, it is less operative in character, and may very possibly
represent a link between the operative masonry of the seventeenth century and the speculative masonry of the eighteenth
century. In support of this suggestion, three points may
be noted:

[1] Transcript and photographic reproduction in Coulthurst and Lawson,
A.Q.C., xlv, 69, and facing 74.
[2] This opinion, expressed by W. H. Rylands in the *Masonic Magazine*,
January, 1882, is shared by Coulthurst and Lawson, *A.Q.C.*, xlv.
[3] Murray Lyon, 160, 161.
[4] *T.C.D. MS.* I, 4, 18. It is printed in the *Transactions of the Lodge of
Research, No. CC, Dublin,* for 1924. It was known to masonic students as
early as 1904 [*A.Q.C.*, xvii (1904), 92].
[5] I have seen only a photostat of the MS., but Dr. J. Gilbart Smyly,
Librarian of Trinity College, Dublin, informs me that the endorsement is in
the same hand and ink as the document itself, and that in his opinion there
can be no doubt of the accuracy of the date.

(i) The endorsement on the MS. is "Free Masonry Feb: 1711," though the term "Free Masonry" was rarely applied to the operative art, even in England.

(ii) Whereas operative masonry, so far as the Mason Word was concerned, apparently recognized only two classes of mason, viz., either entered apprentices and fellowcrafts, or fellowcrafts and masters, this MS. distinguishes three classes, viz., entered apprentices, fellow craftsmen, and masters, each with its own secrets. It is the earliest-known MS. to make such a distinction. The probability is that during the early part of the eighteenth century, before Grand Lodges were formed and firmly established, a trigradal system developed gradually and independently in different parts of the country, by a division of the original entered apprentice ceremony, to form what ultimately became the First and Second Degree ceremonies. Brother Lionel Vibert, in his Prestonian Lecture for 1925,[1] discussed this development, which he suggested took place in London about 1725. The reference in the *Graham MS.* of 1726 to being "entered, passed and raised and conformed by 3 several Lodges" implies that three distinct ceremonies existed by 1726 in that district (probably the North of England) to which the *Graham MS.* belonged. It may quite well be that three distinct ceremonies existed there at an earlier date. Just as the surviving MSS. show considerable differences in the test questions and answers, and in the signs and words, so they indicate differences in the number of ceremonies. The *Edinburgh Register House* and *Sloane MSS.* refer to two ceremonies, the *Trinity College, Dublin* and *Graham MSS.* to three. Such differences are not astonishing, as no uniformity should be looked for before Grand Lodges were firmly established and capable of exercising a unifying influence.

(iii) The history of the document suggests the possibility that the MS. had a non-operative origin. The manuscript is contained in one of the volumes of collected papers of Sir Thomas Molyneux (1661–1733), a famous Dublin doctor and scientist, and, in the opinion of Dr. J. Gilbart Smyly,

---

[1] *The Development of the Trigradal System.* See also his paper "The Second Degree: A Theory," *A.Q.C.*, xxxix.

Librarian of Trinity College, Dublin,[1] was quite possibly written by Molyneux. As the earliest reference to a Lodge of Freemasons in Ireland relates to Trinity College, Dublin, in 1688,[2] it is conceivable that there was a Lodge in Dublin in 1711, although no reference to freemasonry in Ireland in the first two decades of the eighteenth century can be traced.[3] If such a Lodge existed, Molyneux may well have belonged to it.

INFLUENCE OF THE MASON WORD ON MASONIC CEREMONIES

Whether or not the *Trinity College, Dublin MS.* represents a first link in one line of evolution of operative into speculative masonry, I am satisfied that the nucleus of the present First and Third Degree ceremonies can clearly be traced back to the somewhat crude usages and phrases associated before the end of the seventeenth century with the giving of the Mason Word. It apparently grew under speculative influence during the eighteenth century, until it developed into complete ceremonies. This was probably brought about partly by elaborating the content of the ceremonies, partly by embellishing the wording of the ritual, partly by laying more stress on some matters, such as the fidelity of Hiram in refusing to betray the secrets of a master mason, and less stress on others, such as the attempt to obtain a secret from a dead body, and partly by dropping or modifying operative rules and regulations, and developing instead moral teachings, veiled in allegory and illustrated by symbols.

The process of expansion and evolution apparently went

[1] Expressed in a letter written to me, 23 November 1937, in reply to certain questions.

[2] Lepper and Crossle, *History of the Grand Lodge . . . of Ireland*, 36. The late Bro. Chetwode Crawley discovered this reference to Irish masonry in a Trinity College, Dublin Manuscript (*T.C.D. MS.* I, 5, 1), a Tripos [i.e. satirical speech] at the commencements of the University of Dublin, 11 July 1688. He announced his discovery in his Introduction to Sadler's *Masonic Reprints and Revelations*. Dr. J. Gilbert Smyly informs me that it is published in full by Dr. John Barrett in an *Essay on the earlier part of the Life of Swift*, and in Jonathan Swift, *Works*, edited by Sir W. Scott, vol. vi, pp. 226–60.

[3] Lepper and Crossle, 41.

on right through the eighteenth century. I have no intention, however, of attempting to trace that development, a
subject to which Bro. Vibert devoted considerable attention
in his Prestonian Lecture. I shall content myself with
observing that a great elaboration must have taken place
by the last quarter of the eighteenth century, when William
Preston, in successive editions of his *Illustrations of Masonry*,
wrote his commentary on the then existing masonic ritual.
It was probably not until after the union of the two Grand
Lodges in 1813 that our ceremonies attained to something
approximating to their present form. By that time, the
influence exercised by the Mason Word had receded so
much into the background, as to be in danger of being
entirely overlooked. My endeavour in this lecture has been
to give it the recognition which, in my opinion, it deserves.

INDEX

INDEX

Masons—*continued*
expenses defrayed, 48
free and unfree, 50–2
food and drink supplied, 38, 39
gloves, 42–3
holidays, 41–2
hours of labour, 40–1
impressment, 48–9
lodging provided, 39
organisation, 60–72
payment during illness and accidents, 33
"pensions", 16, 17, 33
promotion, 32
recruitment, 47–50
share in civic government, 66
terms of appointment, 32, 33
tools, 41
wages, 34–40
working in quarry, 27
Masonry Dissected, 95
Mason Word:
age, 101–5
conferred by lodge, 63
form of giving, 84
genesis, 57–60, 75
influence on masonic ceremonies, 108–9
more than a mere word, 80–1
object, 86
practical importance, 101
purpose, 59–60
scope, 102
Scottish origin, 101, 104
THE, 100
Master Mason, 15–20, 23
Master of Fabric, 23
Master of Work, 20–4, 53, 54
Master of Works Accounts, 10, 20
Master's Part, 104
Matchpin, 98
Meekren, R. J., 45 n.
Melrose, 48, 49, 63 n., 88
Melrose MS. No. 2, 58
Merlioun, Walter, 17
Métier libre, 70, 71
Métier juré, 70, 71
Miller, Hugh, 11 n.

Milton, 100
Molyneux, Sir Thomas, 107, 108
Motte, 8
Murray, Sir James, 21
Mylne, John, 11 n., 16, 17 n., 18, 19, 22, 25, 26, 66
Mylne, Robert, 13, 14, 17 n., 18, 26
Mylne, R. S., 3

Necromancy, 97
Noah, 93, 94, 96, 97, 100, 103
Nycholay, Sir James, 21 n.

Old Charges, 79, 85, 85 n.
Old stone used, 14, 15
Omnium Gatherum, 65 n.
Organisation among masons, 60–72
Organisation of building operations, 9–15
Overseer, 19, 21, 22, 48

Panmure House, x, 12 n., 13 n., 14, 19, 39, 40, 47, 61
Patten, Andrew, 90
Peebles, John of, 23
"Pensions", 16, 17, 33
Perth, 16, 55, 62, 65 n., 87
Plans, 21, 22, 24–6
Poole, Rev. Herbert, 80
Postures, 84, 86, 91, 102, 103
Preston, William, 109
Prestoun, Robert, 66
Privileged companies, 68–72

Quarries, quarriers, 26–8, 74

Ravelston Quarry, 28
Recruitment of masons, 47–50
Regius MS., 79 n., 90
Ritchie, John, 16
Roslin, Lairds of, 81
Ross, Thomas, 3
Roytell (Roitell), John, 17 n., 18
Roy, Nicholas, 17 n.

St. Andrews:
College, 5, 11 n., 15, 20 n., 25, 27, 28, 42

113

INDEX

Printed in Great Britain by Butler & Tanner Ltd., Frome and London

By DOUGLAS KNOOP and G. P. JONES

THE MEDIAEVAL MASON :

AN ECONOMIC HISTORY OF ENGLISH STONE BUILDING IN THE LATER MIDDLE AGES AND EARLY MODERN TIMES

Demy 8vo., pp. xii + 294. 12/6 *net*

For the historian, a study of an industry probably the second largest in the Middle Ages: for the architect, a discussion of the problems of building in the heyday of Gothic and in the period of the Renaissance; for the "speculative" mason, a realist account of his operative predecessors; and for the general reader, a description of the life and work of the craftsmen and officials who erected the castles and cathedrals of mediaeval England.

. . . a work of much interest and importance on a side of economic history which has been too much neglected in the past.—*Times Literary Supplement.*

A first-rate book and one that is almost as valuable to art historians as to economists.—*The New Statesman.*

Messrs. Knoop and Jones contribute some magnificent spadework to the archæology of Gothic Architecture.—*Journal of the R.I.B.A.*

One can fairly say that their account of the organisation of the mediaeval building industry is the best we have yet had.—*Manchester Guardian.*

This is what many of us have been waiting for; and it will be long before it can be superseded. To the historian of British mediaeval art it will be indispensable; and it forms a valuable chapter in the history of labour.—*Listener.*

CONTENTS:—The Administration of Mediaeval Building Operations—The Organisation of Mediaeval Building Operations—The Medieval Mason —Conditions of Employment in the Middle Ages—Organisation of Masons in the Middle Ages—Two Centuries of Transition—Appendices—Index.

Manchester University Press
8–10 *Wright Street, Manchester,* 15

By *DOUGLAS KNOOP, G. P. JONES* and
DOUGLAS HAMER

THE TWO EARLIEST
MASONIC MSS.

The *Regius MS*. (B.M. Bibl. Reg. 17 A1)
The *Cooke MS*. (B.M. Add. MS. 23198)

Medium 8vo, cloth, pp. vii + 216. 12/6 *net*

Freemasons have long regarded as an invaluable part of their heritage from mediaeval masonry the two manuscripts printed in this volume. The MSS., containing the history and rules of his craft, were for the mediaeval mason very much what the *Carta Caritatis* was for the Cistercian monk, or the Rule of St. Francis for the wandering Grey Friar. Besides being indispensable for the historical study of freemasonry, the MSS. are of interest both to students of building history and students of Middle English Literature. This edition has been published because various previous editions are now difficult to procure, and a good deal of knowledge has accumulated since the time of their last editors.

CONTENTS:—Content and Authorship—Character of the Contemporary Industry—The Assembly or Congregation—The Articles and Points—The Seven Liberal Arts—Hermes and Euclid—The Two Pillars—The *Quatuor Coronati*—The Manuscripts—Related Manuscripts—The Prosody of the *Regius* Poem—The Dialects of the MSS.—Treatment of the Texts—Specimen Pages of the MSS.—Texts—Notes—Glossary—Index.

"The book is provided with all the apparatus that one looks for in a scholarly edition: the introduction and explanatory notes are excellent, and there is a helpful glossary."—*English Historical Review*.

". . . a work of outstanding importance with regard to Masonic history and philosophy."—*The Connoisseur*.

"The present edition will meet all the needs of critical scholarship in the aspects of history, philology and folklore that are involved in these materials."—*American Economic Review*.

Manchester University Press
8–10 *Wright Street, Manchester*, 15

By DOUGLAS KNOOP *and* G. P. JONES

AN INTRODUCTION
TO FREEMASONRY

Crown 8vo., pp. vii + 136. 3/6 *net*

In this little book the authors re-examine, in the light of recent research, two of the most interesting problems in the history of English building—the Origin of Freemasonry and the Connection between Operative and Speculative Masonry. In the first essay, the authors continue their partnership in the study of building history and draw on the results of their past investigations; the second consists of an address given by Douglas Knoop to the Quatuor Coronati Lodge of Freemasons, No. 2076, London, on the occasion of his installation as Master on 8th November, 1935. It was printed for private circulation the following month, and is reprinted here unaltered.

CONTENTS

"This little book contributes much to the critical establishment of the primary outlines of the history of operative and speculative masonry."—*American Economic Review.*

"The non-masonic architect, as well as the initiated, will find this book absorbing, learned and enlightening."—*R.I.B.A. Journal.*

"This book marks a genuine advancement in masonic knowledge."—*Economic History Review.*

Manchester University Press
8–10 *Wright Street, Manchester,* 15

By *DOUGLAS KNOOP* and *G. P. JONES*

THE LONDON MASON
IN THE SEVENTEENTH
CENTURY

Pp. iv + 92. Paper Boards. 5/- net

THE LONDON MASON IN THE SEVENTEENTH CENTURY is based primarily on the records of the Masons' Company and deals with operative masonry in the London area at the period when speculative masonry can first be traced there.

SUMMARY OF CONTENTS

INTRODUCTION.

SOURCES.

THE MASONS' COMPANY. 1. The Monopoly of Trade: "foreign masons": masons free of other Companies. 2. The search for false work.

CLASSES OF MASONS. 1. " Shopkeepers" and Statuaries. 2. Stone Merchants. 3. Overseers. 4. Mason-contractors. 5. Journeymen. 6. Apprentices.

SHORT BIBLIOGRAPHY.

APPENDICES. General Searches of April, 1678, September, 1694 and May, 1696. List of Foreigners and of Foreign Members. Statistics of Journeymen and Apprentices.

" . . . has the merit and interest that one has come to expect of the authors of *The Mediaeval Mason.* . . . Not the least valuable portion of their work is in the extensive appendices, which contain much of the material on which they have based their conclusions."—*English Historical Review.*

" . . . this brief, but important, essay . . . provides an admirable example of that type of local history which must be the foundation for most of our broader economic history."—*Economic History.*

" . . . an indispensable addition to the history of building economics." —*R.I.B.A. Journal.*

Manchester University Press
8–10 *Wright Street, Manchester,* 15